Celestial Conversations

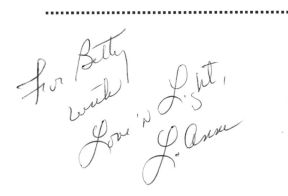

For Betty
with
Love 'n Light,
Jo Anne

Praise for Celestial Conversations

Mental health is fostered by supportive, loving, continued bonds with loved ones, and journal writing enhances growth as well. Lo Anne Mayer chronicles how combining the two can be a powerful tool for healing the past, coping with the present, and preparing for the future.

— **Dianne Arcangel**
author of *Afterlife Encounters*

Celestial Conversations is one of the most remarkable chronicles of its kind to emerge in recent years. Much evidence is emerging from consciousness research that survival of bodily death is real. This book helps confirm that evidence at the transpersonal level. Read and be inspired.

— **Larry Dossey, M.D.**
author of *The Power of Premonitions* and
Reinventing Medicine

In this beautifully crafted book, Lo Anne Mayer shares her story as she would with a friend. The narrative is compelling, and the voice in the telling is genuine and generous.

— **Susan M. Tiberghien**
author of *Looking for Gold: A Year
in Jungian Analysis*

Celestial Conversations provides a fascinating approach to the facilitation of after-death communications. Lo Anne Mayer's new, promising method does not require building a psychomanteum or finding a highly trained therapist. Instead she requires only the right frame of mind, a pen, and paper.

— Allan Botkin, Psy.D.
author of *Induced After Death Communication: A New Therapy for Healing Grief and Trauma*

In *Celestial Conversations*, Lo Anne Mayer continues her relationships with deceased loved ones by journaling with them. The process opened her to a two-way channel of communication that led to the knowledge we survive our physical deaths and healed her grief. Those who seek their own connections will be inspired.

— Robert Ginsberg
co-founder and vice president of
Forever Family Foundation

This is the touching story of a woman who channeled the spirits of her mother and her daughter to heal her family's wounds.

— Arthur Hastings, Ph.D.
director of William James Center for
Consciousness Studies

This book is a confirmation that the Spirit goes on and on, improving with every lifetime, and that love never dies. It will greatly comfort many who mourn losses of ones dear to them as well as those who never had the opportunity to mend breaches prior to their passing.

—Reverend Alma Daniel
co-author of *Ask Your Angels*

Celestial Conversations

....

Healing Relationships After Death

By Lo Anne Mayer

Foreword by Graham Maxey

CΔPE
HOUSE
CAPE HOUSE BOOKS
ALLENDALE, NEW JERSEY

CELESTIAL CONVERSATIONS
Healing Relationships After Death

Copyright © 2011 Lo Anne Mayer

ISBN-10: 193912901X
ISBN-13: 978-1-939129-01-7

Cape House Books™
PO Box 200
Allendale, NJ 07401-0200

www.CapeHouseBooks.com

Cover and book design by Bill Ash

Cataloging in Publication Data

Mayer, Lo Anne.
Celestial Conversations: Healing Relationships After Death/by
Lo Anne Mater ; Foreword by Graham Maxey, M.Div., M.A., 1st
edition

       p. cm.

ISBN-10: 193912901X
ISBN-13: 978-1-939129-01-7

1. Memoir 2. Grief—Spirituality 3. Family life—United States
4. Jounaling

BM645.M7K87 2012
158.1028ma

1 2 3 4 5 6 7 8 9 10

This book is dedicated to my husband, Ray, my love and best friend for fifty years. He experienced this story firsthand with all its hills and valleys. His encouragement and support made all the difference in the birth of *Celestial Conversations*.

There are two ways to live your life — one is as though nothing is a miracle, the other is as though everything is a miracle.

— Albert Einstein

For those who believe, no proof is necessary. For those who do not believe, no proof is possible.

— Stuart Chase

TABLE OF
Contents

Foreword

Celestial Conversations is good news from the front of our human struggle to overcome our hurts, fears, and isolation. It is a remarkable reminder to look for peace even in places our society may not yet help us understand but which our hearts tell us to explore, anyway.

When I first read Lo Anne Mayer's book, something felt very familiar about it. Writing letters to loved ones who had died, and expecting answers, is a very old human practice. Ancient Egypt produced a body of literature in which the living express their thoughts to the deceased, inquire how they are doing, ask for favors, and, most of all, request continued contact. Some of the Egyptian tombs of the common people featured small symbolic doors at which surviving family members and friends came to gather and sit as they awaited a visit with their deceased loved one.

All over the world people have been communicating with the dead as long as writing has existed, and probably much longer. Only recently in human history has it been questioned whether this actually is possible.

As Lo Anne Mayer explains in her wonderfully engaging style, after-death communication is not only possible but capable of healing relationships that could not be mended in earthly conversations. She also makes clear that after-death communication can answer soul-searing questions about the departed that allow grief to do its transformative work instead of becoming an emotional abyss disallowing all joy.

Praying, meditating, and then journaling is the discipline that Lo Anne Mayer has used to extend her conversations with her mother and her daughter after their deaths. All relationships demand a discipline to continue. If we don't seek out the other person regularly with the intent to connect with them in a meaningful way, the relationship dries up and eventually may go away.

In my thirty years working as a psychotherapist, many of my clients have had to go back to relationships with people who have died to resolve issues that seemed forever frozen in place at the point where the other person stopped breathing. For years, I did empty chair work with clients. They would sit in one chair and address their deceased loved one as if he or she were sitting in another. Then they would change chairs and speak as the person they had addressed. Many times new perspectives were gained in this exercise. When speaking as their deceased loved ones, clients regularly uttered things that surprised them. With a puzzled look on their faces, they would say, "I didn't expect her to say that, but it felt genuine."

Similarly, Lo Anne Mayer tells us that although she was doing all the writing in her journals, she found that some of the things "written" by her mother and daughter were not what she would have expected them to say. Not based on her experiences with them before they died, anyway. The messages she received were authenticated by the feelings she had about them.

In 2006 I learned Dr. Allan Botkin's technique of Induced After-Death Communication therapy, which starts with an important setup—pushing aside whatever guilt or anger surrounds a death by focusing on what Botkin calls "the core sadness" of the event. Then, using elements from Eye Movement Desensitization and Reprocessing (EMDR) therapy, that sadness is processed and reduced in intensity at a remarkable rate. From that point it is a very short step to asking the deceased a question, or making a declarative statement, and immediately sensing some form of definitive and important contact that moves the relationship to a new place and sets the stage for its continuation.

One thing that particularly struck me about Lo Anne Mayer's first conversation with her mother after she died was her focus: she did not concentrate on her anger, which seemed very justified, but instead on what she wanted from her mother. In that way, she instinctively did what we do in IADC—focus on the sadness. When that is resolved, anger and guilt go away on their own. They are secondary emotions. The problem is not the hurt but rather the sadness about the hurt.

The starting point of all these techniques is using a discipline with intent. *Celestial Conversations* shows that this process is open to anyone who would heal their past, enliven their present, and anticipate their future without fear. In all cases it is true that death ends a life, not a relationship. Lo Anne Mayer's story documents that the relationship has two continuing parts even though only one party has a live body. It also points to the reality that love, even when seemingly thwarted by circumstance, is never defeated. If it has to wait a lifetime to be revealed, it can and it will.

I recently heard an archeologist/anthropologist explain that the Neanderthal race actually had a brain comparable in size to our own. Yet there is no evidence that Neanderthal society made any important advances in all the tens of thousands of years it existed. Discovery and innovation were almost unknown to Neanderthals. That lack of advancement meant they could not compete with Homo sapiens and eventually went extinct.

Neanderthal vocal physiology, which did not allow them to make as many sounds as Homo sapiens, may have contributed to their demise. Perhaps they did not have as many words and so could not pass along as much experience. Lacking the communication of experience, the Neanderthals were only able to know collectively what each individual could uncover for himself or herself. As a species, then, they could not make any progress.

We already have most of the words we need to talk about after-death communication. What we have lacked is the will and courage to use them so that we all can collectively benefit. *Celestial Conversations* is a demonstration of the courage we need to articulate what we know, which has the potential to revolutionize the way we do almost everything.

— Graham Maxey, M.Div., M.A.
www.lovebeyondlife.com

Licensed Professional Counselor Graham Maxey is in private psychotherapy practice at Inquire Within Counseling and Development Center (www.inquirewithin.net) in Arlington, Texas. He also is associate director of the Center for Grief and Traumatic Loss (www.induced-adc.com) in Lincolnshire, Illinois.

Preface

My mother's death in 2004 appeared to mark the end of my lifelong unsuccessful attempts to communicate with her intimately. Her name was Lois Janes. She was a child of the Depression who grew up to marry a West Point cadet in 1939, just as Hitler marched into Poland. My mother's fear-based Catholic faith became her anchor in wartime and her albatross twelve years later when my father divorced her. Since Catholicism did not permit divorce, Mother could not find comfort by participating in church sacraments or talking to her priest. Judged by her friends, family, and culture as a divorcée, she slipped into a long and silent depression.

Mother decided against therapy, as did many people in the 1950s, and so was left with deep pain she could or would not express. I can't recall one instance when she shared how she felt about anything. At least not with me. Her lack of trust in general, and of me in particular, grew worse with each passing year. My hope of ever having an intimate connection seemed to die when she did.

Witnessing my mother's beautiful death left me overwhelmed and confused. I longed to know how she had turned from a terrified woman into a peaceful angel in a few hours. Most of all, I needed to understand why she felt she could never trust her only daughter.

Those questions haunted me for months after she died. One day I found an old journal of mine written in 1976 to unravel problems one of our sons was having in first grade. Back then I took a course in meditation and journaling. My teacher was a Dominican nun who encouraged our class to pray, then meditate, before writing whatever words came into our minds. Desperate to help our son, I tried this unusual approach to find answers.

Ray Jr. was our fifth child. Though I was a seasoned mother of four other grade school children, I couldn't figure out how to help him with his studies. Trying the nun's approach for one year helped me uncover a number of impediments to Ray Jr.'s achievement in school. The journal writing encouraged everything from giving him extra hugs to exploring his learning disabilities and allergy issues. Each day I prayed for guidance, meditated to clear my mind, and put pen to paper, writing words that seemed to imprint themselves on my mind. When there were no more words to write, I read the page. If the writing had suggested any action, I followed through.

My son's eye muscle problems and allergies were discovered and addressed. We hired a special teacher trained in learning disabilities and discovered another elementary school with the optimal environment for our son. One year after I started journaling, Ray Jr. was healthy and doing well in school. I stopped writing, never certain how the information flowed through my pen onto the journal pages. I felt the Good Lord and Ray Jr.'s guardian angel had guided me. Most important, the method helped bridge my son to a happy life. He never had another problem in school.

The memory of that success inspired me to think about trying the formula again after my mother died. For more than thirty years, I had studied healing and metaphysics. I knew life after death was well documented and that the noetic sciences and quantum physics were part of the new understanding of the universe. I was trained in Reiki, Therapeutic Touch, meditation and angelology. The works of Edgar Cayce, Dr. Raymond Moody, Dr. Deepak Chopra, and Louise Hay were as familiar to me as the Bible. The thought of talking with my dead mother did not intimidate me.

On February 22, 2005, after everyone had left the house, I sat in my favorite living room chair and, with hope in my heart, wrote in my journal:

> *Hi Mom,*
>
> *This letter comes from the certainty that you have a different perspective now that you have escaped your broken body and fearful mind.*

If she wanted to "talk" with me, she would. I had nothing to lose. So began six years of celestial conversations. Little did I know Mother would prepare me to converse with our daughter, Cyndi, who would die five months after I began transpersonal journaling with her grandmother. Eventually Mother answered all my questions, and my understanding of unconditional mother love grew exponentially. This process enabled me to forgive my mother and myself for not knowing how to connect in life. These heavenly correspondences also have taught me karma does not require physical rebirth. I have learned there are many ways for souls to connect.

I share this story in the hope you might open your own celestial conversations to complete your healing with a loved one who has passed on.

Lo Anne K. Mayer
Convent Station, NJ

Celestial Conversations

CHAPTER ONE

The Death

The nurse who called from the nursing home spoke with a soft Jamaican accent. "Come right away, Mrs. Mayer," she said. "Your mother is dying."

I didn't believe her. I was a trained hospice volunteer. I would know if my own mother was dying, wouldn't I? Nevertheless, I raced to her bedside and sat holding her hand for hours that February afternoon. Her demeanor was unchanged. Mother shook from head to toe, as she had for months, though Parkinson's disease was never diagnosed. Everyone who knew her was aware that the Angel of Death terrified her. Sleet tapping on her window broke the silence in the room. When I turned to look at the storm I pondered the effects of the three hip surgeries Mother had endured the past two years.

"I am here, Mom," I said. She turned her head toward the sound of my voice, but then looked to the upper right-hand corner of the ceiling and mumbled incoherently. Time and again, I said, "Mom, I am here. Is there anything I can do?" Time and again, she looked at me with unseeing eyes and, still mumbling, resumed gazing at the ceiling.

Finally, I stood up and leaned over her body, thinking I could make sense of her garble if I put my face near hers. No luck. Mother just moved her head left and right in an effort to keep the upper right-hand corner of the ceiling in her view. I sat down just as the door opened. Mary, Mother's caregiver, walked in. Normally her sparkling green eyes and freckled face lit up the room. Not today.

"Did the nurse call you, too?" I asked.

"No, this is my usual visiting time. What's happening?" she asked in her Irish brogue as she moved closer to Mother's bedside.

"The nurse says she's dying," I whispered. "I have been here for hours. The only difference I can see is that her attention is riveted on the ceiling. She won't talk to me, but I know she knows I'm here."

Mary raised her right eyebrow. Without a word she took off her brown wool coat and threw it in the corner. Then she pulled up a chair on the other side of Mother's bed. Her auburn hair was wet and curly from the snow. She spoke to Mother loudly.

"Lois, it's Mary. How are you?" When she got no response, she took Mother's hand in her own and tried again, even louder. "Lois, it's Mary."

Mother turned directly to Mary and mouthed some words. Her gaze darted back and forth and her expression changed. She seemed eager and excited. Then she returned her gaze to the ceiling, as if referring to something or someone.

"What's happening?" I asked.

I knew Mary would know. She spent lots of time with her clients in the continuing care facility where Mother lived. Her tall, strong body and take-charge attitude made everyone feel safe. She knew Mother well after five years of being her chauffeur, gofer, caretaker, and friend. If Mother were dying, Mary would know. She placed her hands under Mother's blanket and felt around. Moments passed before she instructed me to do the same.

"Place your hands on your Mom's feet, Lo Anne." I followed her direction. Mother's icy feet made me shiver. The room temperature was at least 80 degrees. "Move your hands slowly up to her stomach, stopping at her calves, knees, and thighs on your way." Mother's body felt warmer and warmer as I moved up toward her heart.

My quizzical look prompted Mary to whisper, "The outer extremities shut down first. She is leaving, Lo Anne. I am sorry."

"What should I do?" I whispered. My heart raced. Suddenly Mother, still intently looking upward, attempted to rise from her bed. Her 86-year-old face lost the hundreds of wrinkles so evident a moment earlier. Aglow with joy, she clearly said, "Oh, oh, oh!"

I jerked forward, thinking she would fall from bed. But she seemed suspended in the air at a 45-degree angle for a moment. Then she lay back gently and died. No struggle, no gurgling sound. My mother simply closed her eyes and died with a soft smile on her face.

"What just happened?" I whispered.

"She's gone," Mary replied.

My heart beat wildly as I sat holding Mother's hand. I'd been waiting for struggle and negative drama, but she simply had gone to sleep. I was numb with shock.

My thoughts drifted to my attempts to get my uncommunicative mother to talk with me about her life experiences and feelings. She had stonewalled me my entire life. When she'd moved from independent living to continuing care, I tried even harder to connect with her. Still, she refused to talk about her feelings. In fact, her mistrust of me became insurmountable and her suspicions more bizarre. Mother's fear of the "getcha God" was so overwhelming that she literally shook from head to toe. At the same time, her mouth would close so tightly that her lips turned blue. Sometimes she would blurt out, "If only I could cry."

I remember asking, "What would you cry about, Mom? Can you tell me?"

"I don't really know, dear." That was her favorite mantra when she didn't want to talk about something. Why had my mother become so secretive? The question alternately infuriated and saddened me to the point of tears. After she had drawn her last breath, I recognized my questions never would be answered.

As I held Mother's hand, I mentally questioned her. *Why wouldn't you talk with me, Mom? I am your only daughter. Even now, you hold the secret of your beautiful death. I was right here, but I am totally confused. All I know is that it's too late.*

Mary stood up and announced she would tell the nurses' station what happened. Silently, she picked up her coat and walked out of the room. It didn't occur to me to thank her for being there. My eyes were dry but I could not stop looking at my dead mother. The phone rang, jolting me. On the other end was my husband's voice.

"Are you OK?" he asked. "It's past dinnertime. What's going on?"

I cradled Mother's hand as I responded. "Oh God, Ray, she's dead. I was right here with her. It was mysterious and beautiful, not at all the death we expected. She just went to sleep."

"I should have come. You shouldn't have been alone. I'm so sorry."

"I wasn't alone, honey. Really, it's OK. Mary was here, and I think there were other angelic visitors as well."

"Should I come now?"

"No. There's nothing left to do here. Could you call the kids and my brother and Aunt Marilyn? I am getting ready to come home. I'll call you before I get on the highway."

"Are you sure? The roads are icy, and you must be exhausted."

"Yes, I'm sure. There is nothing left to do. It's over."

As I hung up the phone, I looked even more closely at Mother's peaceful face. I reached out to touch her hair. It was thin and white, like a halo. I was relieved for her but so very sad.

"Now I will never understand what caused the tension between us," I said. Then I inwardly chastised myself. *Why didn't I look in the direction of the upper right-hand corner of the ceiling? Maybe I would have seen something, too.* As a hospice volunteer, I knew there was a lot of data about the dying seeing loved ones or an angel or a light. I'd even met people who described their personal experience to me. *How could I have forgotten that?*

The phone rang again. "It's me." The sound of my brother's voice helped ground me. I needed to tell Jack the story in minute detail.

"Jack, do you remember how terrified she was when she talked about her death?"

"Sure do, and how many rosaries she broke praying that God would let her into heaven," he sighed. "Such a waste of worry and regret."

"Well, it wasn't like that at all." I told him everything. "Jack, Mom's been dead almost two hours and those wrinkles haven't come back to her face. She still has that serene look."

"Unbelievable! It's a far cry from the death I thought you would describe. You know, I knew she was gone before Ray called. I don't know how to describe it, but I think she came to say goodbye. I plan to be on the next plane from Hamburg. I'll call you when I land."

As I hung up the phone, I wondered if Jack thought I was crazy. He knew my metaphysical beliefs. I was happy Mary had been with me. She could testify to the truth of my words. The door of Mother's room opened and the night nurse entered with her medication.

"My mother is dead," I announced.

"What? No screaming?" he replied, setting down the medicine tray and moving closer to the bed. "It's not possible!"

"Trust me, she's dead," I reiterated, not wanting him to touch her. He looked at me, then at her, turned on the overhead light, and reached to take her pulse.

"She's dead. I don't believe it!" He picked up the tray and walked out.

A chapel-like quiet settled over the room again. It was close to 10 p.m., time to go. "Is there anything else I can do, Mom?" I asked. Out of habit, I waited for her to say, "Could you hand me my mail, dear?" Or, "Could you water the plants before you go?" All the old excuses she used to keep me in the room when I wanted to leave. The silence was terrible. The overhead light illuminated her unlined face and any thought I held in my heart that it was all a big mistake disappeared. I put on my coat, picked up my gloves and purse, and left.

The hallway was silent and dark except for the sound of my heels clicking on the floor and the news on someone's television. I walked toward the nurses' station. The Asian nurse spoke softly, "I am so sorry for your loss. Don't worry. We will take care of everything."

"Do I need to sign something?" I asked.

"No, ma'am. Drive carefully. The roads are quite slick."

I nodded and headed for the elevator. I stepped in and stood for a few moments before realizing I hadn't pressed the ground-floor button.

When I'd scraped the ice off my windshield and steered my car slowly onto the road, I took one last look at the continuing care facility. It loomed in the night like an aircraft carrier at port. My mother had decided to move there without my help or even my awareness, but that was nothing new. She had sold her large home and her vacation home in Canada without consulting me or my husband, and we didn't know she'd purchased a new townhouse until the sale was under contract.

Snow swirled around my car like the memories in my mind. How surprised and delighted Ray and I had been when Mother, still deciding whether to move out of the townhouse and into assisted living, invited us to visit the facility. During our inspection, she peppered us with questions: "Do you think this place is right for me? What do you think of the apartments? Should I check their fiscal history? What about the town of Denville? Do you think anyone will visit me?" What I didn't realize was that we were the last in a long line of "advisors" who already had given their opinions.

"I just don't know what to do," she whimpered, twisting the handkerchief in her hands.

As we walked the halls, stopping at rooms along the way, Ray and I were impressed, even enthusiastic. It met every criteria we thought Mother needed. We praised her for her research, confirmed her choice, and offered to do whatever we could to help.

"Mom, you couldn't ask for a better place," I oozed. "You have friends living here already. Your doctors are across the street. The hospital is next door. There are two Catholic churches within a mile, and the town is charming. The apartment you selected is bright and beautiful. Even the view of the golf course from the huge deck is spectacular. You can't beat this!"

"You won't have any trouble selling your condo," Ray added, "and we can help with anything you might need. This is perfect."

"So you think I should sign the contract?" Mother asked.

"Absolutely!"

Without further discussion, she led the way to the manager's office. We witnessed her signature, never realizing the contract and manager had been in the office waiting for our arrival. As we drove home Ray and I chatted happily about her decision. Mother was silent. After we dropped her off at her townhouse, Ray and I continued our assessment.

"She must be mellowing," I said. "Can you believe she actually wanted us to give an opinion and be part of this historic day? A change in the wind?"

"Maybe things will lighten up now," Ray replied. "She will really need us from now on."

A week later one of our children phoned to tell us Mother had called a secret meeting of her grandchildren to complain that she needed their help.

"Your parents are putting me in a home," she told them. Feeling shocked and betrayed once again, I confronted her and demanded to know why she had done such a thing.

"I don't really know, dear," she cooed.

"Of course, you know, Mom. I'm the one who doesn't know. You told our kids that Ray and I were forcing you into continuing care. That is an outrageous lie! Why in the world would you do that?"

"I don't really know, dear," she responded, staring at the floor. "I guess I got scared."

"Even if that were true, why wouldn't you discuss it with me? I am your daughter. Why would you call a meeting of my children and blame Ray and me for your own decision? It's crazy! What were you thinking?"

"I don't really know, dear. I just don't know."

"How many times have I heard that pathetic response? I am done, Mom. You really are a piece of work. Don't ask for any help from me. I am so tired of this manipulative behavior that I could vomit." I slammed the door on the way out.

I didn't follow through on my threat. I helped her sell her townhouse and move into the continuing care facility. The whole time Mother, playing the sorrowful old woman, thanked me profusely. But never once did she apologize for calling her grandchildren together to rescue her from the "old folks' home."

Hot tears flowed down my cheeks as I pulled into our driveway and hit the garage door opener. My husband stood at the doorway with a drink for me in his hand.

"You made it," he said. "Thank God. I was worried when you didn't call."

I apologized and sat at our kitchen table sipping my drink. I repeated everything I could recall about Mother's last hours. As I spoke, Ray fixed me something to eat, turning to look at me in surprise from time to time.

"What do you think she was looking at?" he asked.

"How I wish I had turned around to look at that damn ceiling. It just never occurred to me. I couldn't take my eyes off her." Silence settled over us as I picked at my food.

"Ray, do you remember when Mom almost died last year after her hip surgery?"

"How could I forget?" he said. "When we walked into that post-op, all the monitors were going crazy, and the nurses were sure she was dying."

"I can remember taking Mother's hand and telling her to sit by the lake in Canada and watch the loons. I told her over and over to relax by Newboro

Lake and be at peace. Before long, all the monitors returned to normal."

"It was amazing, Lo Anne," Ray went on, enfolding my hand. "She literally came back from the grave in those moments. Did she ever tell you what she remembered of that near-death experience?"

"I wish. I tried many times to follow up on that night. I reminded her of my conversation with your dad about his near-death experience, and how that led me to discover so many books about the subject. I shared all I learned in hospice training. But she would never respond to my questions or comment about her personal experience. It certainly didn't change her terror about dying the way it did for your father, and that makes her peaceful death all the more puzzling. God, I wish I could ask her what happened."

Seeing my exhaustion, Ray gently encouraged me to save my questions for another time.

"Go to bed, honey," he said. "Tomorrow is going to be busy."

Nodding, I hugged him and headed for our bedroom. As I slipped under the covers, I remembered those last words, "Oh, Oh, Oh," and the last look on my Mother's face. *I'll never forget that look*, I thought as my mind faded to black.

CHAPTER TWO

Unfinished Business

Mother's funeral Mass, held in the parish church she loved for fifty years, was a blur to me. Forty years earlier, Ray and I were married there. I knew every detail. But that day my mind drifted. I was grateful my brother and our children took the main roles in the ceremonial part of the funeral. Through my exhaustion, I watched the rituals as if they were a movie and reflected on my memories. When the soloist sang the first words of the final hymn, *On Eagles' Wings*, my tears began to fall. I was defeated. We were on the way to bury my mother.

We piled into the limousine. I held the cross from her casket as the funeral procession drove past her home on its way to the mausoleum. As I stared out the window at the gray winter day, my mind drifted to when Mother asked me to accompany her to this very burial place. She'd wanted my opinion.

"Do you think anyone will come visit me here?" she whispered.

"We will come wherever you are buried, Mom," I said. "Do you really think you want to spend this much money?"

"This way, rain or snow won't keep you from coming," she replied.

"We will come, I promise. This is a big decision, Mom. How do you feel about it? Is it scary?"

"I don't really know, dear. I just need to do this." Silent and determined, she'd proceeded to the cemetery office to sign the papers for the mausoleum.

The burial service was short because of the frigid February weather. Mother's body was placed in the open slot in the wall. Everyone's breath was visible as the priest said the final blessing. He stood next to an altar that would be used if we ever wanted to have a Mass celebrated there. Mother must have considered that.

Everyone rushed to their cars and onward to the reception where the room, with its crystal chandeliers and snow-covered glass roof, seemed surreal to me. There I learned a new secret. Mother had a second cemetery plot in another town next to my stepfather's grave. Apparently she felt God wouldn't approve of her being buried next to her second husband. Playing continuously at the reception was a video our daughter Karen had produced and narrated for her grandmother's eightieth birthday. The film was a beautiful reminder of Mother's many talents and abilities. In it Karen described her grandmother as a "gracious lady who had the ability to make anyone feel safe." My brother, Jack, born six years after me, claimed that he had no idea as he grew up that money was tight.

But there certainly was a monetary crisis. My father was a serviceman stationed in Korea with little money or inclination to pay alimony. When his telegram arrived asking for the divorce, Mother reeled. Looking back, I think she may have assumed she was being notified of his death, not the death of their marriage. Her parents paid for an attorney. She didn't demand my father's financial help and refused to fight the divorce, but she was so crushed and depressed that she did nothing at all for months.

Finally Mother recognized she hardly had a penny to her name, no credit, and two children to support. We moved to a garage apartment on her parents' property, and she found a job. To establish her own credit, she bought a refrigerator. Jack and I were put in separate schools. She was determined to begin her life as a single parent. Money, or lack of it, was never discussed.

Two years later Mother married her boss and, with little warning or discussion, we moved into his home. I went to the Catholic high school Mother selected. Jack went to a Catholic grammar school. Within a year we moved into a new, larger home that Jack and I learned about only after it had been purchased. I remained at the same high school, but he was put in a prominent private boys' school. No one mentioned the cost. Somehow we had moved out of poverty into the upper middle class without ever discussing finances. It was such a smooth transition that my brother never felt a bump in the road.

Mother learned to invest under my stepfather's tutelage. She was his star pupil. When she died, she left a sizable generation-skipping trust for her grandchildren. I was never consulted about the trust. She hired professionals. Even when I offered to help pay her monthly bills as she got older, she said she preferred to hire a secretary. How Mother spent her money was none of my business.

In Karen's video all the grandchildren gushed over the one-on-one magical birthday trips their grandmother had planned for them. She took them to a toy store and bought them elegant dinners at her country club. In her home she even designated a room that contained a dollhouse for each of the six children. In the summertime she took them to her home in Canada. They loved it all. They loved her. No one did grandmothering better than Lois Janes.

In the video her nieces said they admired Mother's thirst for education. Though she never went to college, she read books on philosophy and metaphysics. Her niece Nancy exclaimed, "I am reading *People* magazine and Aunt Lois is reading about noetic science." Mother's social success was applauded as well. She was president of a prestigious garden club, and she established a Parents of Alumni Club at my brother's private high school. Though a member of all the most prominent organizations, she never lost the innate ability to chat, as it is said, with "paupers and kings."

Mother's love of reading was matched by her love of travel. Restricted to the United States as a young woman because of the Depression and World War II, she made up for it when she grew older, traveling to the Caribbean, Canada, and Europe as often as she could. Most of her incentive was to be with my brother, Jack, who spends a great deal of his life in Germany. Her other reason for travel was a genuine love of culture. When she couldn't travel outside the States, Mother went weekly to Manhattan to visit museums or to Lincoln Center to take in an opera or performance of the New York City Ballet.

The video also made it clear that many people admired Mother's religious faith. She was a mentor for my cousin who was filmed saying, "She was always there for me. She is my hero." As I watched, I recognized all the traits attributed to my mother with a tinge of jealousy. I only knew these endearing qualities through the eyes and words of others. I thought, *How did we miss each other on the road of life, Mom?*

Her wisdom, however, was a big part of my life. When I needed to find a high school or doctor for our children, she always could find the right information. When I needed nutritional information during my pregnancies or when the children suffered with allergies, Mother knew the perfect book or specialist. She even introduced me to astrology by having my chart done for me, followed by one for my husband and each of our children. Intrigued by metaphysics, she shared what she learned. Then, fearful we both might go to hell for seeking the knowledge we found, she stood back. We could discuss anything but her personal feelings and private business. That was sacred ground forbidden to me.

I scrutinized the birthday video for even a hint of Mother's religious fears. There wasn't one. So many people told stories about her that surprised me. For instance, though I'd been close to one of my cousins all my life, I never knew she shared a spiritual bond with my mother. I only knew that years earlier Mother had included her in a family trip to a shrine of the Blessed Mother in Lourdes. At the time I didn't understand why Mother had asked my cousin to join us.

Mother truly was appreciated and admired. But did anyone really know her? It was difficult to tell. I certainly didn't. I gazed around the crowded room and felt as if I were looking at a hundred pieces of the moving puzzle that was my mother's life. Everyone knew a piece of Lois Janes. Would I ever understand her? Did it matter anymore?

Two days after the burial, we were summoned to my mother's lawyer's office for the reading of her will. As we drove, my stomach turned as I remembered the last time I was there.

Mother had invited me to lunch. It had taken me months to recover from her clandestine meeting with my children about putting her in a home. Eager to heal the tension between us, I was ready to consider the lunch as a peace offering. I regaled her with stories about the children, which almost made the visit fun for me. As I reached for the check, Mom asked if we could stop at her lawyer's office on the way home.

"I have to sign some papers," she said. "Shouldn't take a minute."

The request was surprising, but I was determined not to ask any personal questions. I wanted to keep the atmosphere as light as possible to continue our truce. After I was introduced to Mother's lawyer, I followed the two of them down a hallway to a conference room and a large round walnut table with two sets of papers on top. Gently seating Mother in front of one set, the Chanel-suited lawyer nodded to me to sit in front of the other. Mother said nothing.

"We need to update your mother's will, Lo Anne," the lawyer said. "If you could read and then sign by the X on all four pages, that will take care of everything."

"Mom?" I asked, turning toward her. She looked away. My voice grew stronger. "What exactly am I signing?"

The lawyer put her hand on my mother's shoulder as she responded to my question. "It's very straightforward," she replied. "Your Mom made a decision she would like to rectify. It is a simple change, as you can see when you read and sign the papers."

I stared at my mother and then turned my attention to the papers. Certain I had misunderstood the wording, I read them again. "Reinstate?" I asked. "Am I being reinstated into your will, Mom?" I looked directly into my mother's eyes. She looked everywhere but at me. "Mom, what in the world is this?"

The lawyer restated her position, "As I said before, your Mom wants to update her will. As soon as you sign the papers, we can get you on your way."

My heart pounded furiously as I spit out the next question. "Mom, don't you think an explanation is in order?"

"I don't really know, dear," she whispered. We sat in silence until the lawyer suggested Mother and I might want to be alone. She left the room. I turned my chair to face my mother, who looked like a fox caught by hound dogs.

"Well?" I asked. For fifteen minutes, I waited for any kind of explanation.

"I don't really know, dear," she finally said. "Let's not spoil our beautiful lunch."

I let the reality of what happened sink in. Stunned and disgusted, I picked up the pen, signed all four pages, and rushed from the office. I punched the elevator button, got on, and never looked back. By the time the elevator hit ground level and I unlocked my car, tears were rolling down my cheeks. I sat in the driver's seat, my thoughts churning, *My mother had taken me out of her will. Why? What had prompted that? And why did she want to put me back now?* The whole thing made no sense. I wanted to scream.

At first I didn't hear the tap on the passenger side window. An insistent rap caught my attention. It was Mother. I nodded my head. She climbed in and shut the door. Before she finished buckling her seatbelt, I zoomed out of the parking lot. At a stop sign the first of many questions fell from my lips, "What were you thinking? What made you do such a thing? Why didn't you warn me about what was going to happen at the lawyer's office? Why in the world did you take me out of your will in the first place? This time you've gone too far."

By the time I parked in front of her house twenty minutes later, I was out of words. To every single question came the same answer, "I don't really know, dear."

My head ached. I waited for her to open the passenger door, looking straight ahead and making no attempt to help. As she stood beside the open car door, she spoke her final words. "I am so sorry that you are upset, dear. You always make everything so dramatic. It really isn't that big of a deal, Lo Anne."

Oh, but it was a big deal. I felt stabbed in the heart by my own mother. It took me months to be able to speak to her again. Even then, there was no explanation or apology.

Six years later, there I was in that same office with that same Chanel-draped lawyer at the same walnut table listening to my mother's will being read. I would not have been surprised to discover I had been removed from the will again. But I hadn't been. During the hour-long conference, I only heard a few words. My mind was lost in memories. There still was so much unfinished business between the two of us, still so much pain.

What wasted effort, I thought. *There'd never been a chance of healing our relationship. I am 64 years old and*

I never got close to intimacy with my mother. Maybe now if God asks you for an explanation, Mother, you won't be able to get away with your favorite reply.

Months passed without my truly grieving my mother's death. Our family needed lots of help. Our nine-month-old grandson was stricken with cancer. Another grandson was diagnosed with autism. Our son-in-law endured three life-threatening operations. Our daughter Cyndi began divorce proceedings. One of our sons was getting married, while another was getting divorced. I pushed my grief aside to help the living. If I thought of Mother at all, it was with defeat and regret.

CHAPTER THREE

Through the Veil

One year after Mother's death, I was cleaning out a bookcase when one of my journals from the 1970s fell on the floor. I skimmed it, remembering how I'd combined meditation and journaling to tap into divine guidance. The technique had helped me at the time to unravel our six-year-old son's academic difficulties. *Could this formula of prayer, meditation, and journaling help me heal the grief I feel over the loss of my mother?* I figured it couldn't hurt to try.

The next morning I sat in my quiet living room, said a prayer for guidance, and meditated to clear my mind. Then I placed a new journal on my lap, picked up a pen, breathed deeply, and wrote on the first page:

> *This journal was purchased to connect with my Mother, Lois Janes, after her death on February 5, 2004. The purpose is to heal our relationship after her death and before my own.*
>
> *Lo Anne Mayer*
> *2/21/05*

I set the book on the table and pondered what I was about to do. *Will it work? What if it does? What if it doesn't?* The phone rang. I didn't write that day.

My resolve quickened the next day. I took the phone off the hook as a sign to the universe I was intent upon beginning my quest. I placed the journal next to me, prayed for guidance, and meditated for twenty minutes. I wanted to be open to a possible connection without distractions. Then I picked up my pen, dated the page, and wrote:

> *2/22/05*
>
> *Hi Mom!*
>
> *This letter comes from the certainty that you have different perspectives now that you have escaped your broken body and fearful mind. I recognize that I was not dealing with you as a whole person over the last few years that I was the caretaker of record. I see now that you were trapped in your situation like an animal hit by a car. I understand more clearly that you were fighting for your life. Your seeming attacks at me were more an effort*

*to survive. I am sorry I didn't recognize that
when you were alive. It would have made those
last years less of a nightmare for both of us.*

*This letter is written in the hope that we can open
up a dialogue that will bring us closer in time. I
miss the wisdom you used to share. I miss your
listening ear. I don't miss your physical self yet,
because you hurt me so much in your physical
state.*

*However, I do believe that conversation through
writing can help us both to soothe the pain and
open up immense possibilities in the
transpersonal state.*

*If you are willing, I have questions that need
answers. I have confusion about my present state.
I could use your advice about moving to a new
home. I also thank you for putting money aside
for the children. No one could have guessed that
Cyndi would have been the first to need that
money. It has made such a difference. She could
use your help as well. She is so like you. If you
could use her dream-state to advise her, I would
be grateful. I would also take that as a report that
our communication has begun.*

*Love,
Lo Anne*

I put down the pen and closed the journal, plac-
ing it on the table as if it were made of porcelain. I
didn't tell anyone what I was doing. Three days
later, I picked up the journal a third time. The house

was quiet. Beginning again with prayer, then meditation, I wrote:

2/25/05

Dear Loanne,

I am grateful for this venue. We do need to communicate and I have tried without success to get through in other ways. Your judgment and anger are powerful barriers to what you want to do. Forgiveness is the only way to open the door of communicating. I ask (beg) your forgiveness for my mistakes in communicating with you over the years. Communication was never my strong suit, even in the best of times. I know toward the end of my life, I made a great mess of my communication. In your kindness, please overlook those years. They really were not me, nor my intentions. I got lost and couldn't find my way back. I took any hand, listened to anyone (but you and Jack), and paid anyone to lead me out of the darkness. So much wasted time. So many wasted judgments. I so regret those years.

Now I see that you know that communication and love can be shared transpersonally. We have another chance to be lovingly communicating. It is exciting to be given another chance. I can help you and the children and the grandchildren. I am just as interested and close to you all as I was on earth. There is one big difference. I am clear. I can see the potential. I can see the obstacles. I know how to be helpful. This is a good way to begin to chat. Thank you for forgiving me enough to try.

The first thing I want to compliment you on (after opening this door) is turning to God for guidance. I was afraid to listen to God's guidance. Keep that up. You are surrounded by help. Listening is the secret, followed by trusting that guidance. Another deficit of mine. Trust never came to me, as you often said. I trust you now and I trust you to do the right thing. A miracle in itself.

Lovingly,
Mother

I made no attempt to edit or punctuate. Word for word, I wrote exactly what I heard in my mind. I didn't read the page until the words stopped flowing. Then I read it several times. Carefully, almost ceremoniously, I placed both journal and pen on the table.

"My God, it is working," I said aloud. My heart raced. Mother and I had begun to communicate. I had no doubt the letter from my mother was the contact I had hoped for. If I hadn't journaled in this manner years ago, I might have stopped after my hand scrawled "Loanne." My mother always had written my name in that manner. For fifty years I had written "Lo Anne." For me, the spelling was a sign Mother was writing through my pen onto the paper.

I needed a couple of days to comprehend a holy exchange had taken place and, though I desperately wanted to tell someone about it, I didn't. The divine thread seemed so precious, like my mother's death. *Maybe it was a fluke*, I thought. For several days I allowed the busyness of life to distract me. Then I was drawn back to the journal.

On February 28, 2005, I tried again. And then every few days, for years. The writing became ever more easy in sessions that took on an aura of sacred ritual. Gradually, I didn't concentrate on the formula as much as the intention of getting in touch with my mother. The ritual of prayer, meditation, and writing became fluid. I asked her questions as if she were on the telephone or we were emailing. Our subject matter varied from my fears about my children's lives to her description of her new understanding and perspective from the other side of the veil:

> *3/16/05*
>
> *Dear Loanne,*
>
> *You are noticing our connection and it brings me great hope and joy to recognize the possibilities of this new (and better) relationship that lies ahead of us. I wish I could tell you how wonderful it is to be in a place (non-physical and transpersonal) that gives me utter joy. So unlike my human personality. All barriers are gone. All goals are wide open. No time or physical limitations. It is just fantastic! I am so happy!*

Mother held nothing back. Neither good news nor bad. She didn't always answer my questions directly or right away. Sometimes she addressed obstacles she felt I needed to remove so I could understand her advice, which often was wrapped in references to her own life. Other times she spoke of subjects that were the furthest from my mind. One day, when I was attending a writers' conference at Skidmore College, she bluntly told me I needed to change. She pointed out I had patterns of behavior that were hurting me and would cause problems in the future.

6/21/05

Here you are, Loanne, at Skidmore, following your guidance without reservation. How I wish I had done that more! In so many ways you have always been ahead of me, as it should be. Children should always surpass their parents. Sixty-three, going on sixty-four. Let me tell you that my life at sixty-four was very similar emotionally to yours. I too was frightened. I was also very alone. My husband (your stepfather) had died and I felt alienated from everyone, including you. My perception of life was in error. I just didn't have the tools I needed to move forward. You do. You have spent years learning how to release old beliefs. This will serve you well. You are shedding your skin, like a snake. The new skin is underneath.

As you observed yesterday, it is a rebirth. It is a

necessary rebirth. Time to put it all together. Your gifts and talents, your appreciation for your life and that includes your mis-takes. This is a precarious time that needs focus and concentration, not regret or anger. Anger is, as you put it, a genetic deficit. Your father and I used anger as our barometer for life.

You need to recognize that you carry our ways, our patterns. You can see what that does to your children. It is hard to see yourself. However, if you can release your own anger, it will also demonstrate to your family how to release their genetic defects, too. Teach by example.

I am praying for you and the family. I am watching closely. I am seeing a very loving, courageous daughter whose only problem is how to take time for herself. You will make the time. I promise to help and then you will help millions in your final years.

Love,
Mother

I knew I was filled with regret that Mother and I hadn't truly connected in life. Deep down I also knew I was angry about family situations. However, I didn't see the "genetic defect" of anger, as she put it, until I reread her letter. She opened my eyes to the truth. Mother also complimented me on living and thinking in ways that were "braver" than her own. For instance, she applauded my efforts to become a more evolved soul.

10/30/05

Dear Loanne,

You are amazing in your constant striving to be more, do more and love more. Your focus on God, on good, is so important to your life-goals. I am proud of you as your mother and teacher. You are keeping God as your north star, whether it is in your personal life, your family life, your social life or whatever comes to you "by accident." You have absorbed the message. Congratulations!

You are even recognizing your judgments and criticisms for what they are: barriers to love. I never got that! Again I congratulate you. The knee-jerk tendency is there but you recognize it. You are growing spiritually.

Don't forget to be kind to yourself. Don't judge and criticize yourself either. That is more difficult, I know. I taught you so well, but I didn't know what I was doing. The agenda of your life really is love. You do so naturally, just like Ethan (your newest grandson). Ethan is you! Not just Michael's son. He is you: free, fun, full of curiosity and love. As you spend time with him, don't linger on regrets for what you did or didn't do for his father, look at Ethan's innocence and remember your own. That truly is how God looks at you, with love and pride and so do I!

Lovingly,
Mother

All her advice was timely, sequential and loving. As months and pages flew by, I realized Mother's human negativity and criticism had disappeared. All that was left was the light of her soul and warmth of her love. Though her answers were generous and pointed, there was one time she curiously evaded my question. Or so it seemed to me. I'd asked if my father had died yet. When my parents divorced, my father remarried, started a new family, and cut himself off from Jack and me for the rest of our lives. Mother wrote:

9/11/05

You asked about your father. We have been "in touch," and he does have many regrets, as do I. You know, honey, when we come to Earth, we have so many intentions and plans for the journey. Sort of like when you get married. You have an idea of what life will be like, but you don't really know how you will react until you get into the middle of it. When you live out your life you have an intention, and then there is reality. Your father's intention, as was mine, was to be a healer. He tried, but wound up a warrior: A reluctant warrior. He was undone by that at a soul level. However, we spawned two healers in our children. Healers who are far more effective than we were. From here we can be proud of you.

At the time I was disappointed with the answer. I thought our celestial conversations had allowed us to talk about anything, including what my brother referred to as the "black box" of her first marriage.

But a week later my mother's friend, married to a classmate of my father, called to tell me my father had died. When I looked at the date of my journal, I discovered it coincided with the date of his death. When Mother said, "We have been in touch," she wasn't kidding.

When most of my personal questions had been answered, the journals took on new subjects, such as life and death and the karma of souls. Sometimes Mother's messages were related to me and our family, sometimes not. Through the next few chapters, I share some of her unsolicited observations, which could help heal any mother-daughter bond, or any unresolved relationship.

First, Mother insists anyone can reach through the veil to the other side when both parties are willing. One day she wrote through me:

11/09/05

Forgive everyone as quickly as you can. Make it your primary purpose of each day. Forgiveness is the key to the door of unconditional love.

Love,
Mother

From her first letter she let me know my own unwillingness to forgive—my anger and exhaustion—had made it impossible for me to hear her when she tried to reach me from the other side.

Mother emphasizes that judgments, criticisms, re-sentments, and guilt put up barriers to communica-tion among the living and between the living and the dead. Once she saw the power of forgiveness from the other side, she wanted me to know about it.

Typically, she balanced her heavy communica-tions by pointing out good things she noticed, as in this letter:

3/23/05

Dear Loanne,

Your motherhood skills are just wonderful. You don't see what I see, but you flow from one to the other with the ease of an eagle and eyeing things from afar. Then swooping down with incredible timing to deal with whatever situation is at hand.

You will really enjoy the Life Review after you die, when you will see the incredible ways you have served your children. Times you weren't tuned in, for whatever reason, will be an astounding small percentage, compared to the times you were. Let go of the guilt! It killed me unnecessarily. It distorted my view of life and kept me in a constant state of depression. Let it go. You have nothing to regret. You did the best you could with the understanding you had at the time. (Are you laughing?) Those words of your teacher, Louise Hay, came from me. Well, they are the truth. I can see that clearly now. All you need to do is focus on the gifts of your children, the strength of the family bond, and the time you have to gather your life experience, wisdom and loving support into one great picture of The Now and The Future. Do not waste time on guilt, regret, judgment, and criticism.

You told me. Now I beg you. Don't waste time. It's so precious. I feel that I wore you out. Forgive me. I know better now. I am helping. I can be in many places at once now. I am clear in my vision and in my instruction. I am enjoying my experience immensely. To use your own words, "It's going to be all right."

Love Always,
Mother

Nothing in Mother's words could have seemed more out of sync to me. My life was in chaos. Some of our children were experiencing marital difficulties. Also, an inspection had uncovered serious environmental issues with a home on which my husband and I had made an offer. I felt overwhelmed and exhausted.

Mother helped by sharing how she got lost in her own victimhood when she was alive. But she was in a position to help me now:

4/15/06

I got lost then, but I am not lost now. I am really delighted with our teamwork. It is so much easier from here. Loanne. Everything is easy. Everything is clear. Everything is loving. There is no fear. It is truly wonderful to be so free again.

Our comfort level with journaling grew with each passing month. I found writing in the journal a bit like writing another language in that I struggled to incorporate the basic messages into my everyday life. I forced myself to say "Forgive me" more often, as Mother instructed in her letters. My tendency to blame others became more evident to me. I began to see my day-to-day resentments through her spiritual eyes. Mother was leading me toward the world of forgiveness, but the path was filled with minefields. At that time I had no idea I was being groomed to tackle the most challenging moment of my life.

CHAPTER FOUR

The Big Shock

A s I continued journaling with Mother, the problems in my life grew worse. My daughter Cyndi was heading to court to work through a complicated divorce. One of my sons remarried. We walked away from the house of our dreams that we had found after two years of looking. In my frustration I turned to Mother, who responded in this unusual way:

4/20/07

You are getting a glimpse of my pain and aloneness, but don't take it to heart, just recognize it as a way we can connect now. I am in such a good place of understanding now. I see that much, if not all, of my pain came as a result of my judgment of situations and people. I really reaped what I sowed. That is your lesson.

Stay true to the Course in Miracles, the teachings of Jesus and Mary, and Gandhi. No attack is justified. No judgment is clear.

No decision based on self-defense is worthwhile. I finally got that toward the end. Turn everything over to God. He has the power and the plan that gives our lives meaning. He knows what is best, but we so often get in the way, and zig when we should zag. Just turn it over, even if it seems to be a movie stuck on rewind. Turn over every thought, every hope, every situation to God and you will feel better. The outcome will be perfect and on time.

Lovingly,
Mother

Around that time a friend told me about a writing workshop in Glastonbury, England.

"The workshop leader is the one you loved so much at Skidmore," she told me. "I'll go if you go. What do you think?"

She dangled the tantalizing question in front of me on a day I truly wanted to run away from home. My mind drifted to Camelot and the beauty of England in July. Ray encouraged me.

"It will be good for you," he said. "You need a break. You've been helping everyone, and it's only going to get worse. Go for it. It wraps up your love for travel and writing in one package. Besides, it's only one week."

Karen, our oldest daughter, called that night to say she was being sent to London on assignment at the very same time. "It's a sign, Mom," she said. "The last time we were in London was when I was attending Oxford. Maybe we could meet there for a little walk down memory lane."

I made the arrangements and found myself immersed in a women's writing retreat in the magical world of fairies and the mystic Isle of Avalon, the legendary island of the Arthurian myths where it is said King Arthur recuperated from battle wounds. Ever since I saw the stage production of *Camelot* on Broadway, I adored the story of King Arthur and Queen Guinevere.

Lodged at the Abbey House in Glastonbury, I peered out the windows of the walnut-paneled library to the cemetery ruins in the back—the very cemetery where King Arthur, as well as many saints of the British Isles, are said to be buried. I also climbed Glastonbury Tor, a hill in the middle of the Summerland Meadows where only one structure stands—the roofless St. Michael's Tower, an ancient monument. Enchanted by the view, I squinted to actually see the mists of Avalon. Glastonbury seemed to be a doorway between the worlds of fact and imagination, heaven and earth, life and death.

After several days of exploring and writing, I called Ray to share my adventures and thank him for encouraging me to come. He was visiting our daughter Diane while I was away. Using all the British change I thought I'd need for a quick update, I dialed the number. The moment I heard my daughter's voice, I bubbled with excitement and launched into an account of my walk through Stonehenge and discoveries at the Chalice Well at the foot of Glastonbury Tor. Diane interrupted me three times.

"Mom, listen to me," she said, her voice crackling on the line. But I rattled on with enthusiastic joy. "Mom, we've been trying to reach you. You need to come home right away. Cyndi is dead and Dad—." The phone cut her off.

I knew I couldn't have heard that right. I sat, stunned, and said to the woman waiting in line for the phone, "She said my daughter is dead?" I couldn't move. I stared at the phone. Jane gave me all her change.

"Call back right away," she said. I did. Ray answered on the first ring. Through tears, he described a policeman coming to the door to tell him that Cyndi was found dead in her bed that morning.

"How did she die?" I asked.

"They said she committed suicide," he said. "We called Karen, and she will meet you at the Radisson Edwardian Heathrow Hotel, right at the airport. The rest of the children are flying in. Come home."

All I could say was, "I'll call you from the airport hotel."

I hung up but couldn't move. Jane had gone to speak to the manager of the hotel, who ran up the stairs and assured me he would get a taxi to the airport, a hotel room, and change my tickets so I could get home as quickly as possible. All I could do was nod my head.

In that moment I knew what an out-of-body experience was. I knew I should do something, but what? Jane asked if she could help me pack. I stared at her. My mind stopped and then spun so fast that I couldn't think. I needed to be alone. I declined any help and went to my room where I got out the suitcase and collapsed onto the bed in tears.

Collecting myself, I opened the suitcase and threw all my belongings into it. As I was locking the strap around the luggage, Jane came back to tell me the taxi had arrived. My gaze swept the room. I picked up my purse and carefully walked down-stairs. Many of the women in the workshop were standing at the foot of the stairs with tears in their eyes. Several handed me cash, just in case. I couldn't talk.

The Abbey House Hotel manager took my suit-case and gently helped me into the taxi. All I heard was the sound of my own scrambled thoughts.

At the hotel airport I had just enough cash to pay the driver. Thank God for the generosity of the women in Glastonbury. I checked into my room and waited for Karen. Suddenly, I was terrified. The room was too quiet. I went to the lobby to wait. At least there I could distract my crazed thoughts by people-watching. In the crowd I saw Karen's face, pale and pained. Only a year older than Cyndi, she looked just like her sister. As we clung to each other, she whispered, "Now I know why I was sent to London, Mom. God didn't want you to be alone."

We cried together as we walked to our hotel room. Somehow her ticket was changed to match mine so we could sit together on the same plane. Long into the night Karen and I questioned each other, knowing no answer would suffice. Exhausted, we fell asleep.

In the morning we took our seats on the plane. As the engines droned, I looked out the window and in my mind's eye I saw Cyndi's early years. I saw the ease of her birth. She simply slipped out of my body into the hands of the physician. I saw her golden hair and beautiful face. I saw her running with her siblings and opening Christmas presents. I saw the glowing disposition that carried her through so many trials as she grew older. But it was her smile I saw most clearly. I hadn't seen it often since she was a teenager, but she had flashed me one just before I left for England.

The flight attendant interrupted my reverie when she brought dinner. Picking at my food gave me a chance to ask Karen what she was thinking.

Karen's eyes were brimming with tears. Instead of answering me, she changed the subject to what we would do when we arrived home. I hadn't thought of any aspect of the wake or funeral for Cyndi until that moment. Typical of Karen, she made a list of tasks and helped me focus on delegating responsibilities. Not easy for me.

The flight attendant cleared the meal as I ruminated. *How do I bury my child? Where do I begin?* Karen and I talked about what Cyndi would want until the pilot announced our final landing pattern. Bracing myself for the reality of seeing our family and my dead daughter, I got up to go to the bathroom and found the flight attendant.

"Could you help my daughter and me deplane first?" I heard myself ask. "We are going home to bury my daughter."

As my own words hit the air, my knees buckled. Tears flowed down my cheeks. My throat closed. I couldn't breathe.

The flight attendant said she would work out something as I opened the bathroom door and convulsed into tears. I didn't care if anyone could hear my groans. I couldn't stop. The flight attendant knocked on the door to ask if I was all right. It was time to be seated. With compassionate eyes and a soft voice, she led Karen and me to seats near the departure door in first class.

Everything was a blur until we got home. As the airport limousine pulled into our driveway, my children and their spouses poured out our front door. Everyone moved toward the limousine as if they already were in a funeral procession. My husband's face was burgundy from tears and high blood pressure as he wrapped his arms around me. I greedily accepted everyone's hugs. It felt so good to be held and consoled by my family. Amid a sea of tears, I led everyone to the living room for what I hoped would be answers. But there were none. No one knew exactly what had happened.

That night I tossed and turned, berating myself for not being home when Cyndi needed me. Finally, I got up and went to my office. There on the desk was my journal. I decided to ask my mother for help.

7/22/05

Mother, I need help!

I need to know from you that Cyndi is alright. I need to know that you two are together. I need help in processing the unfathomable. Cyndi is dead! Dead! I can't get my head around it! My whole being is numb. I woke up this morning thinking for a second that it was just a bad dream!

The kids have been great. Ray has been remarkable. I felt that he would go to pieces, but he is buoyed by the children. I am grateful. I am grateful for the children's insight, intelligence and consideration. I am grateful to have other children. I am grateful for my faith in God. I am grateful for the fact that Cyndi had a small measure of love in her life.

She almost made it, Mom. She almost got to the end of the divorce to a new day. Help me to surrender, accept, and have faith. Help me to be peace and love and light. Help me to grow with this experience. I want to be more enlightened, not dark. I want to be love, not hate. I want to be all I can be as a soul right now. I need help.

Love,
Loanne

I signed with my girlhood signature. As I put down my pen, I felt as helpless as a baby crying for her mother.

That night I recalled that Cyndi and I had shared many discussions about the Teachings of Abraham, an entity channeled through Esther Hicks who for more than twenty years has taught The Law of Attraction. This universal law emphasizes that we should focus on joy. I bought the tapes and listened to them as well. Cyndi and I had lively conversations about how to use the power of the mind to pivot away from negative thinking. She was particularly interested in the passages about creating a new joy-filled life, even though her life at the time was filled with negative drama. How I loved to watch Cyndi's face light up as she described how she pictured her life after divorce.

A knock on the door brought me back to the moment. My son said he'd made coffee. The troops were up. It was time to face facts and get to work. Karen's list was a huge help with making arrangements. Back home everyone had a job to do. Mine was to pick out Cyndi's grave with our daughter Diane. There's something inherently wrong with selecting a grave for one's child. We chose the same cemetery where Mother was buried. Mother picked a mausoleum. Diane and I found a place next to a statue of Our Lady of Lourdes. Perfect. Cyndi had chosen the name Bernadette for her Confirmation name years ago because she loved the story of Lourdes. I thought, *The Blessed Mother will take care of our daughter.* The place felt exactly right.

We delayed the funeral Mass when government tape tied up our son's passport, making it impossible for him to leave Tokyo for his sister's scheduled funeral. The pastor of our church and the funeral parlor agreed to wait one more day. The business of funeral arrangements insulated me until I fell asleep. The next morning I went back to my journal and wrote Mother's reply:

7/23/05

Dear, dear Loanne,

I am here with Cyndi. She is fine, surprised but fine. Relieved. I am with her, helping her process, loving her and loving you.

She says, "It is just like Abraham said. The cocoon is now a beautiful butterfly."

I know your heart is aching but you are doing a

wonderful job. You are doing everything she asks better than she can imagine. She loves you so, Loanne. There is no anger now, no blame, no regret. She is filled with the light 'n love you wanted for her.

Do not blame yourself or anyone. She sees she wrote her own story. She accepts that with deep wisdom. Paint her final physical story with love and peace and healing. Let that be her legacy. Nothing else matters now. She is fine. She is surrounded by lovelight. Show that now for all to see.

Your purpose is to reflect her light today and tomorrow and the tomorrows to come. She became dark through incorrect decisions on earth but she is a heavenly light now. Reflect her present light like a mirror. You know what I mean.

Love,
Mother

I read and reread my mother's words. I stood up with determination "to reflect her heavenly light." I took a shower and laid out my black pantsuit. Today was the first day of the viewing. The casket would be open. After asking the funeral director to order butterflies that could be released at Cyndi's grave, we were directed to an adjoining room. I said to the family, "Let's do this together. Hold hands and stay close."

When the door to the viewing room opened, the casket seemed miles away. I wasn't sure I could make it all the way there. My legs felt like they were mired in mud. The last time I saw Cyndi she was waving goodbye after a visit at our home. So alive! So beautiful! Forcing myself to move to the coffin, my heart stopped and then pounded wildly at the sight of her. She looked like Sleeping Beauty. I slipped a small statue of an angel into the coffin and leaned to kiss her. Her cheek felt like the stone-cold statue I had just tucked into the velvet lining. My mind split into a million jagged memories. I couldn't think. I couldn't cry. I couldn't help any-one. I couldn't comprehend that I was looking at my dead daughter. The room was silent except for the movement of fourteen human beings struck by death.

The funeral parlor manager whispered in my ear that my grandson was in another room. I found Cyndi's oldest boy sitting alone in a side room, staring out the window.

"Do you want to see your Mom, honey?" I asked. He nodded.

Holding his hand, I slowly walked him into the viewing room. With the whole family surrounding him, he stood in the back staring at his mother's casket. He could not move closer. Witnessing the pain of our thirteen-year-old grandson was excru-ciating.

The funeral director asked us to step out of the room so the casket could be closed and the body moved to a larger room. I was at peace with the closing because Cyndi never liked open caskets. I handed the funeral director a picture of Cyndi. I'd asked a local photographer to lift her individual portrait from a family picture taken on the day Ray and I celebrated our fortieth wedding anniversary. It was a happy day. We were all on our way to Mass, smiling and dressed in our Sunday best.

Before we left the room a large spray of flowers arrived. I always hated to send flowers when someone died, but Cyndi loved her garden. For that reason, the bouquet comforted me. *I must remember that,* I thought, as we proceeded into the large room to receive guests. I took in the pictures the children had gathered and displayed on poster boards. *When did they have time to do all this,* I wondered. My breath caught as my eyes came upon Cyndi's baby picture. With tears in my eyes, I looked at the bouquets and baskets and read the names of friends and family who sent them. No one spoke. I looked at my watch. In five minutes, visitors would arrive.

The closed casket with its floral spray was centered against the far wall in the room. Cyndi's picture was placed on a table next to the kneeler. Looking at my watch again, I implored the family, "Stick together in the receiving line, so we can watch out for one another." I dreaded the first person walking into our silent funereal cave.

Hundreds came. I tried to thank them for their concern, forcing myself to look into the eyes of the next person in line and the next and the next. When one of my sons came by, I asked, "Can you get me some water?" He turned me around. The water bottles were right behind me.

When we broke for dinner, I went directly home and, still in my pantsuit, collapsed onto the bed. Two hours later, Ray awakened me. I hadn't moved. I combed my hair, ate a piece of toast and headed back to the funeral parlor with my family. The line went on forever. That night, I poured myself into bed and willed myself to sleep.

The next morning, before daylight, I sat with my journal. I was not sure I could get through the day. Nevertheless, I wrote:

7/26/2005

Dear Loanne,

We are with you – Cyndi and I – together. With Tillie and Henry and Artie and Kenneth and Mom and Dad and countless others. We surround you with our love and appreciation for who you are and what you represent – love and healing.

The pain of all this grief process is such an opportunity. Forgiveness is the balm. Do not be distracted by blame or anger. Choose the

*forgiveness road no matter what your mind tells
you. Teach by example. There is no other way.*

The thought of my husband's parents, Tillie and
Henry, and my own grandparents, whom I called
Mom and Dad, being with Cyndi was an immediate comfort. Picturing my husband's two brothers,
who were Benedictine priests, comforting our
daughter was a personal blessing. Both Father Kenneth and Father Arthur had been part of Cyndi's
life since she was a baby, but her favorite was her
dear Uncle Artie, who had died ten years earlier.
His death had been a deep loss for her.

Suddenly the energy changed and my hand
wrote:

Mom —

*I love you. I am so sorry to cause you and Daddy
such pain. I never meant to leave. I just hurt so
bad. I wanted to stop the pain. I never wanted to
end my life. Mommy, I am so sorry. Please
forgive me. You and Dad have been so wonderful
all along. I am so grateful to you. I know you
didn't think I really noticed all you did, but I did.
You showed us with your love and your strength.
You gave all you could.*

*I made a tragic mistake. I made many mistakes. I
can't even count the mistakes, but I see your love.
I saw your love through the midst of my pain.
Look for me today. I will show you that I am with
you. Look for me in the butterflies and in my*

*brothers and sisters. Be proud, Mom. You are
everything I hoped to be and I love you so!*

*Love,
Cyndi*

"Dear God!" I cried out. "Could it be? Could
those be Cyndi's words? Am I hallucinating? Is
there any truth to any of it? Is it wishful thinking?
Even if it is, I feel the love and I need it now. I will
think about what this means later. I will take the
love and look for Cyndi at her funeral."

I reflected, prayed, and cried until I heard my
husband's knock on the door. I said, "I'm ready."

CHAPTER FIVE

Another Burial

Hundreds of people, most crying, filled the pews for Cyndi's funeral. At one point Cyndi's oldest boy stood next to me.

"Stay close to your uncles after all of you escort your mom's casket down the aisle," I said, kissing the tears brimming in his eyes. His uncles helped him take his place as a pallbearer.

My heart stopped at the sound of the organ music. As I walked down the aisle in the procession, faces popped into my field of vision. My tears fell. My lips trembled. I willed my legs to walk toward the priests waiting at the altar. As we made our way into a pew, my granddaughter Gracie winced, "Grandma, you're squeezing my hand." I had no idea she, or anyone else, was walking with me. I felt totally alone.

The rituals comforted me as I allowed myself to take in the prayers and the candles, the incense and the music. I remembered Mother's words to me that morning in the journal:

> *Do not blame yourself or anyone. She sees she wrote her own story. She accepts that with deep wisdom. Paint her final physical story with love and peace and healing. Let that be her legacy. Nothing else matters now.*

How is that possible? I wondered as I peeked at Cyndi's casket.

When the priest instructed us to reach out in peace to others in the church, I prayed audibly. "Help me, Lord," I said, before walking around Cyndi's casket and crossing the aisle to Cyndi's husband and his family.

"Peace be with you," I said, offering my hand. My husband followed. "Peace be with you," he said. Cyndi's oldest son, flanked by his Uncle Greg and Aunt Crystal, stared at me from the other side of the aisle. His face was the color of white chalk.

After the final prayers of the Mass, Karen read a tribute she'd composed for her sister:

"…Anyone who has found themselves at the receiving end of Cyndi's kindness can tell you that her essence was shown in the little things she did: a warm dry towel waiting for you as you got out of the pool, a hug that held on just a bit longer when you were scared or lonely, the first cup of hot coffee out of the pot when you were exhausted, or a miniature Christmas tree she had made by hand. These are the things that love is really made of.

"For Cyndi, love was in the details. Yet gratitude for any of these gifts almost embarrassed her. Kindness in her view was never something to be earned… it was a fringe benefit you got, just for knowing her. Coming from a big family whose members were always competing for center stage, Cindy was content to dance around the perimeters of the spotlight and lead the applause for everyone else. She was the first to celebrate your successes and be the bandleader for your joy…."

I had never been more proud of Karen. In the silence that followed, I envisioned Cyndi smiling at her sister. The priests walked to the casket for the final blessing. The music started again. I needed all the strength I had to follow Cyndi's casket to the hearse. My heart shattered when Cyndi's oldest son broke down while gallantly trying to help the other pallbearers put the casket in the hearse.

The funeral procession led to the cemetery where Mother had been buried seventeen months earlier. The statue of the Blessed Mother stood sentry duty above Cyndi's empty grave. Mother's crypt was a stone's throw away. I prayed these two powerful women would care for our daughter from now on. My job was done. Or so I thought.

Official prayers were said. I didn't hear a word. But when each of Cyndi's siblings read a poem, my heart trembled along with their voices. The butterflies were brought to me for release. I offered one to Cyndi's family members and each member of the rest of our extended family. In silence all seventy butterflies were released.

Then everyone left the cemetery. In silence we drove to the reception, where our family spread out to thank everyone and share stories. All offers of help were kind and genuine. But what could anyone do? Too tired to talk, we all went home. The children started confirming flights home. I went straight to bed.

Before daylight the next morning, I wrote to Mother:

7/27/05

Dear Mom,

Thanks for your help yesterday. What a day! It was filled with exquisite pain and immense pride and extraordinary healing. I was so proud of my children and grandchildren. I am amazed that I was able to take it all in without the blur of too many tears. Then to find the extraordinary gravesite and the butterflies! Wow! We all worked together – those on earth and those no longer physical. Thanks so much for helping me to go through this whole week seeing the wonders – the miracles – the love. It was so much more than the grief. I know the grief will come in waves, but I am grateful the miracles outshone the grief during the wake and funeral.

Now our children will leave us. Diane will go home, as will Mike and Heather, Greg, and Crystal. I hate to see them go, but I need to have them go. Help Ray and me have a healing day with Ray Jr. It is a brief moment in time before Ray and I are alone with each other and the reality of Cyndi's death. Help us. Pray for us. Ask the angels to enfold us. This is the hardest thing we've ever done as a couple – bar none.

Love,
Loanne (again the signature of a child)

Someone was up. I smelled coffee and headed for the kitchen. Sending off the family members took all my focus and strength as they packed, made phone calls, and said goodbye. We were each being released to walk our own grief journeys. After the last goodbye, I returned to my journal:

7/29/05

Loanne dear,

I feel closer to you now than I have in many, many years. The grief you are sharing with me is a beautiful gift. Your wisdom and intuition are serving you so well. Your strength, your motherhood, your perception, and your faith are such an example to your family and friends. Your broken heart is a gift to your wisdom and humility. You can only learn to receive when you have nowhere to turn, just like me.

When I see all the love and compassion around you, it makes me happy. While I am with you and Cyndi, the physical hug is something I wish I could give you now. Everything has changed in a twinkling of an eye for Cyndi. Her motherhood has been enhanced by death. Her clarity and resolve have been enhanced by death. Her appreciation of the support of her entire family is enhanced by death.

We are all here with her. We helped her through the recognition and regret of her death. We are working with her to soothe and direct her sons. Any hatreds she harbored in life have disappeared like a puff of smoke. She can love her children now as they could never be loved by her on earth.

Truly she is shining like the sun right now. Geared up for her children. Strengthened by those here and there. Clear that her role of mother never ends — only changes for a moment in time.

Love always,
Mother

Now what? I thought. *What do I do now?* I did routine things: changed beds, cleaned the kitchen, ran the wash—all tasks with a beginning and an end, tasks offering the reward of accomplishment. I threw away dried-out flowers, surveyed the food in the refrigerator, and took out the garbage. Exhaustion set in. I napped, but the nightmare of

Cyndi's death woke me up. Surprised to see daylight, I rose and prepared a cup of tea. As I sipped the brew, my eye caught the calendar on the counter and I mused, *What day is it?* Reading the notation for a long-planned visit with our son's family in Lake Tahoe, I gulped. *I can't do that. It's only two weeks from now. I don't have the strength to make the trip.* But a voice inside me suggested otherwise: *Maybe it would be good to have a change of scene.*

"Mom?" I asked aloud. "Is that you?" I found my suitcase in the attic—the same one I used to go to Glastonbury. Then tears overwhelmed me and I went back to bed.

A few days later, I picked up my journal and wrote:

8/1/05

Dear Mom,

I am feeling all kinds of feelings: mostly exhaustion, sometimes love, often anger, even at Cyndi, sometimes a dull ache. I feel as if I am adrift on the sea and the darkness is coming.

Today I will exercise and rest. I will be open to receive the love offered to me. I crave news from the coroner. I am open to be guided by you and all those above who have a clear picture of what's happening. I do not have such a picture, and I don't know when I will, so I depend on others. Help me to be all I can be under the circumstances.

Love,
Loanne

Determined to fill my days with positive action, I answered sympathy cards and phone messages. I checked in with our children to see how they were doing. They said they were OK, but the tone of their voices told me otherwise. Grief is a lonely road. Haphazardly, I selected my wardrobe for Tahoe.

Cyndi's husband agreed I could spend time with Cyndi's youngest son. Picking him up at his home for the first time since Cyndi's death was almost too much for me. I drove onto her driveway and froze at the sight of her door. I could barely breathe as I walked into the kitchen. Throughout our day together I sensed my grandson hoped I would take him to his mother, but he did not ask.

"We'll make another date," I promised. "I'll talk to your Dad."

"OK," he said. I silently promised myself to work out a consistent pattern of visiting as soon as we returned from Lake Tahoe. Yet I had so many questions. I went back to my journal with Mother the next morning:

8/5/05

Dear Loanne,

Yes, this is a test, but not to see if you pass or fail. This is a test of what you truly believe. This is an opportunity to let go of unnecessary beliefs and habits; of looking at where you are and what is best for you now.

Cyndi is just fine. If you think you are surrounded by love, you should "see" her! She is experiencing finally the love she so thirsted for on earth. She is understanding completely that what she wanted (or thought she wanted) cannot be found on earth alone. She wanted to know love completely inside and out, just once. Now she knows love completely – everlastingly. She is glorious in her state right now. Trust me, she is fine.

She is close to her boys and doing everything she can from here (the spirit state) to give all the loving support that they can handle.

Cyndi is grateful for the prayers and Masses being offered for her. They are helping to clear away the confusion that surrounded her once she arrived. As happy as she was to see us all, she thought at first she could return. Confusion and regret set in. Our roles (Artie, Kenneth, Tillie and I) were to love her through the midst of confusion. We worked really well together. You would be surprised and proud. Cyndi is totally wrapped in our love and so are you and Ray.

Love,
Mother

I increasingly depended on my journal for advice. Mother alternately praised and cautioned me to take care of myself. Though I was ever more grateful for our celestial conversations, I told no one else about them. They were my secret weapon of survival and I didn't want to risk anyone's judgment about them.

Ray and I flew to Lake Tahoe and partook of the healing waters there. Our granddaughter Ashley brought up memories of Cyndi as a toddler. I felt as if someone were constantly changing the channel on a television. When I looked at Ashley, I saw Cyndi at the same age. When I held Ashley, I remembered holding Cyndi. Sometimes switching between channels made me dizzy, but mostly I felt grateful for the unconditional love of a lively two-year-old. I missed Cyndi's boys, though. I'd left my journal in New Jersey, too, and missed that connection.

I asked Mother to help me decide whether I should go to Tokyo in October to help our daughter-in-law when her second child was born, as I had long ago promised. I already had the airline ticket.

"Should I leave Ray and Cyndi's boys?" I was tired. Though my husband was encouraging, I felt guilty about leaving. Mother gave this advice:

9/29/05

Dear Loanne,

I know that you are anxious about your family members, but be careful that you don't go down my path of anxiety. Constantly turn over each person, each relationship and each concern to God. Picture it in your mind. Put each concern in

God's capable hands. I used to give my troubles to the Lord and then take them back. It turned into a tug-of-war that ruined my faith in God's help and turned me into a victim of God's power. Worry is so insidious, Loanne. It comes like a thief in the night and steals your strength, your sleep, and your confidence. Take care to hand over each small worry and nip anxiety and depression in the bud!

The tendency to make mountains out of molehills is genetic, but you know better. "I am releasing this person, place or thing to God's care. I relax and know that all is well because God is in charge." I tried to say that, but my mold of fear was too strong. I will remind you constantly of this prayer. It is the only path you want to take.

Ray Jr. and Robin are really glad you are coming. You will be a light of wisdom, love, and healing for them. Your job is to speak softly and with faith. Your job is to be love, not be the judge. Your opportunity is to teach only love.

Love,
Mother

I flew to Tokyo and didn't take the journal. I was still afraid of having to explain my celestial conversations to anyone. While in Japan, however, I seriously considered starting a journal with Cyndi. Several months had passed since she'd jumped into Mother's journal. As soon as I returned from the trip, I purchased another journal and wrote:

11/13/05

This journal is begun with Cyndi after her death to help me process my confusion and grief.

Without hesitation, I said a prayer and meditated to center myself. Then I wrote my first letter to Cyndi because I finally was ready to "hear" what she had to say for herself:

11/13/05

Dear Cyndi,

As the days, weeks, and months go by, I find myself more confused and more grief-stricken than in the beginning. I need your help to understand and to help your sons understand and grow from their grief. Please help me and your father and siblings comprehend and process your choice to die at this time, leaving us all nonplussed and grief-stricken.

Love Always,
Mom

CHAPTER SIX

Healing Pages

Cyndi's death was deemed a suicide, but that wasn't enough for me. Two months before she died she'd finally confided in her father and me that she had an alcohol problem. I'd feared that, but then she'd gotten the help she so desperately needed. She'd been on the right path. Still, she'd been going through a rough time. So I wrote to her asking what happened and she described being distraught that fateful night when she returned to an empty house and contemplated the impending divorce and what life could be like afterwards:

11/17/05

Mommy,

I walked into the house — found more wine and thought about the future: Family Services, court, the boys, all dark thoughts. I longed to hear a sensible word, but couldn't bring myself to call any family member. I called a friend. He didn't answer. I left a message. I called another friend. He leveled me for my drinking at a ballgame that night. I was so ashamed.

In tears I put together the pills but I didn't take them — at least I didn't think I did. I just wanted to go to sleep and put it all behind me for a few hours. I went upstairs. I tried to call them both again, but no answer.

I fell into bed and all of a sudden Grandma was there with Uncle Artie. I was so happy to see Uncle Artie. He made me smile. I wasn't exhausted anymore. We just sat and talked. I talked and Grandma was there and Uncle Artie kept asking questions about the family. Much later I noticed we weren't in my bedroom anymore. I realized that Uncle Artie and Grandma were dead. I began to realize that I was dead and I wanted to run back to my body and my miserable life and my boys.

There is a wall, you know. You can't go back. That's where hell is, Mom, at the wall. You can see what is happening: the police, the discussions about the body — me. You hear the telephone

*conversations with the family. That is where hell
is! I kept yelling. I'm so sorry. I didn't know what
I was doing! I don't remember doing anything!
But no one could hear me. I was in hell.*

*I came to my boys at night and whispered words
of love. They heard that clearly, but they don't
remember.*

*I am so very sorry. I could have said something to
you but I couldn't get the words out. I could have
followed up with just a small confidence, but I
couldn't get the words out. There was nothing
you could have done to keep me from my path of
self-destruction. The drinking and drugs killed
me.*

*Love my children for me, Mom. Hold them.
Cuddle them. Nurture them. Help them to
remember that I love them. Will always love them
and I am with them forever.*

Love,
Cyndi

"She *was* alone in her pain," I yelled. "She had no
one! I should never have gone to England. I could
have saved her. At least I could have been with her
as she died. She was alone, alone, alone."

Of course I knew Cyndi was not alone. Working
in hospice, I'd come across many stories of angels
and guides escorting people through death's door.
And hadn't I seen my own mother's death? If that
experience taught me anything, it was that no one

dies alone. Cyndi even described her uncle and grandmother being with her. But I was not there. I did not hold and love her as she passed — a mother's worst nightmare. Just like any nightmare, it seemed real.

Cyndi wrote again:

11/19/05

Mom,

Please don't waste time blaming yourself or others. The burden of losing me is enough to carry. Don't waste time in this life trying to put the pieces together. Don't blame yourself. Stay in the moment — don't look back or you will turn into a pillar of salt. When we are together again — none of this will matter.

Be easy on yourself and Dad. Compared to my life, you have both been spectacular! We all make mistakes. From my new perspective, none of it matters because we all do the best we can, even those of us who appear to fail. There is no failure in heaven, even though there is no heaven as we thought. There is just love. You can't imagine how good that feels right now — to bathe in love, real love.

Don't waste time, Mom. You don't have it to waste. Look for the light. You are on the right path. Forgiveness is the key. The key to God's world, which is truly wonderful.

I love you more now than I ever did on earth. I

know love now. You are on the right path – follow the light!

Cyndi

Her words inspired me to forgive. I wrote a mantra, "I am willing to forgive _____." I carried it with me. Many times a day I filled in the name of a person who came to mind in the moment. Often I put my own name in the blank. Guilt plagued me. Anger surged through my body, mind, and spirit. Unconditional love seemed an impossible dream.

Cyndi insisted on keeping me focused on loving her sons. In her journal she would not allow blame or judgment to take over one page:

11/21/05

Love heals, Love soothes. Don't be distracted by the dark side.

Intellectually, I knew she was right, but to truly forgive is a challenge. I prayed for help to forgive. I went to Confession, asking for advice on how to forgive everyone involved, including me. I asked others to pray for me. After Ray and I completed a course on grief at our church, I opted for one-on-one grief counseling, choosing a counselor comfortable with metaphysics. After working with her six months, I shared what I was learning through my journals. She encouraged me to continue them because they were clearly helping me.

The counselor introduced me to EMDR, or Eye Movement Desensitization and Reprocessing, a technique developed in 1987 by Dr. Francine Shapiro, a psychologist and senior research fellow at the Mental Research Institute in California. Her technique has been internationally recognized as an effective treatment for people with Post-Traumatic Stress Disorder, which my counselor felt applied to my situation.

"It can help you remove the traumatic memories of Cyndi's life and death," she told me, "and make room for you to focus on your intention to forgive."

She proceeded to help me identify a traumatic thought about Cyndi's death. Not the entire scene, but one aspect of the trauma. I picked one that plagued me with guilt: I was in Glastonbury when Cyndi died. The counselor had me close my eyes and remember the moment I heard about Cyndi's death. Then I picked a number from one to ten to identify the scope of the trauma. Ten blazed vividly in my mind. My throat tightened as I remembered the scene, and I opened my eyes. The counselor tapped on my knees and asked me to follow sets of eye movements until the memory became less disturbing.

"What number comes up?" she asked. To my surprise, nine came up. We repeated the process over and over until the number fell to zero. This slow but steady process worked for me.

I still recall the situation, but I don't feel the trauma anymore. EMDR helped me focus on forgiving myself and gave my body the gift of breathing deeply whenever the thought of that awful day came up. Deeper breathing brought oxygen to my brain, which in turn helped me think more clearly. Piece by piece, thought by thought, I had a tool to release traumatic memories with the help of my counselor.

Ray's physician recommended we join The Compassionate Friends, an organization dedicated to parents who have lost children. The organization's motto, "We need not walk alone," was the answer to my loneliness. Even my friends and family had no idea what to do or say. But when I was with these new "friends," I was certain everyone in the room knew my searing pain because only a person who has lost a child truly can understand the trauma.

Members of our chapter helped me understand the stages of my grief journey—some by their strength or sheer survival, others by their faith or honesty. All were heroes to me. I still attend meetings and remain in awe of the parents who have helped me.

Despite the open sharing among members about the death of our children, I still was reluctant to share my celestial conversations. It took several years before I talked about my journaling with the other parents.

Soon December arrived. With it came a new opportunity. I continued journaling with Mother during the holiday season and, before I knew it, our first Christmas without Cyndi was two days away. Almost every family member had come together in our home to comfort and love one another. Mother encouraged me:

12/23/05

Loanne,

I know that this holiday is difficult — the most difficult gauntlet you have ever walked. Cyndi is sorely missed by all. You can feel it. She can feel it too. What you are going through is what the Church calls Purgatory. Purgatory means regret — deep gut-wrenching regret. Like grief, regret is visceral, even when you don't have a body.

For this holiday, please balance gratitude with regret. Gratitude that you are all together. Regret that Cyndi is not with you. Gratitude that almost everyone could make it home for Christmas. Regret that Cyndi is not here. Gratitude that you had forty years with Cyndi. Regret that it could not be more. Gratitude that you took advantage of every opportunity to tell Cyndi that you were proud of her courage and loved her deeply while she was alive. Regret that you didn't say more. Gratitude that Cyndi left her boys to love. Regret that Cyndi can't physically love them.

Gratitude balances grief, Loanne. Gratitude

balances life on earth and beyond. I know. I am grateful for the incredible family you and Ray produced and I am grateful to finally spend quality time with Cyndi.

Love,
Mother

I don't know where I got the time or courage, but I journaled with Cyndi as well on Christmas Day:

12/25/05

Mom,

Do not doubt for one moment that I am in the midst of our family. I am immersed in their joy at being together and bathing in the warmth of their love for each other.

I was so lucky to be part of our family. I didn't see that as completely on earth as I did when I came to this state of awareness. Everything is clearer and each detail jumps out at me. I can't miss the wonder of having been part of our family. We are an intense bunch. We are so strong and so beautiful. I wish you could see what I see, Mom. You and Dad did such a great job with us. We were a handful. Like a bunch of wild stallions. It is a wonder you survived the parental role. But you did more than survive. You gave us more than you will ever know on earth. I can't wait to stand with you when you review the investment of your love in us.

The only message I have for the family at

Christmas is to love more. Love each other more. Love those you call enemies. Love is never wasted. Speak your love. Treasure your love. Don't waste time on anything that is not love. Love is all there is and time is awasting for all.

I love you and I am happy to discover that love is all you take with you into this dimension. Then love shines through all that has occurred on earth. Like sparkling diamonds, Love is all there is. Hear me. Love is all there is! If I never told you how much I love you, remember that my love for you grows as I watch from here. My family is amazing and my love showers you like the raindrops now and forever.

Merry Christmas!

Cyndi

That message inspired me to share my journals with family members for the first time as we were eating. I spoke to our children about the journaling that I had begun with their grandmother. Intrigued I was writing down words that my mother had imprinted on my mind, no one expressed doubt. Perhaps they'd heard my metaphysical conviction for so long that it did not seem impossible to them that I could be reaching out to my dead mother. Our son Michael was curious as to how it worked.

"Do you hear Grandma talking, Mom?"

"No, it's more like feeling the words in my head. No voice at all. I write word for word, but I don't read the whole page until there are no more words to write. If I try to read the words as I go along, I lose everything."

Diane was curious as to how I knew that it was her grandma.

"I can feel her in a way, Di. The way the words flow, I just know it is her, although sometimes the metaphysical language is not the language she used when she was alive. There is an energy that feels like Grandma, too, and it's far different than the energy I feel with Cyndi's journal."

Everyone at the table stared at me. "Yes, I am also journaling with Cyndi," I explained. "It's been very helpful for me to talk with her. Maybe you would like to read the journals so that you can see for yourself."

Without a hesitation, Greg said, "I would. Where are they?"

"Me, too," Karen added.

"They are in my office, but let's finish dinner first," I said. "Anyone who wants to look at them, feel free. I'd love your thoughts on them, if you would like to share."

As dessert was served, we talked about Christmas memories, but not so much about Cyndi. After dinner we cleared the table and did the dishes. At first we didn't notice our son Greg had disappeared into my office. He came into the kitchen with one of my journals in his hand.

"Mom, I have been reading your journal with Grandma. This is really amazing stuff," he said. "Do you know that your handwriting looks different when you write Grandma's words, than when you write your own letters?"

"Show me."

Greg showed me the pages, but I couldn't see the difference. Nevertheless, I was thrilled that he not only wanted to know what I was doing but found the journals a positive experience.

"My turn," Karen said as she scurried down the hall to my office with the journal she'd pried out of her younger brother's hand.

Throughout the night the children and I had lots of discussion about the journaling. No one expressed doubts that I was in contact with their grandmother and sister, but no one asked me to teach them how to do it. When I suggested they might want to learn how to do their own journaling, no one was interested.

After the holidays I felt like a smashed crystal. Mother offered help:

12/28/05

Loanne,

You are so tired. You are bone tired. Your emotions are at the raw stage. Float. Remember how you like to float on the lake — any water? Do so now. When swimming through life gets too much, just turn over and float. Watch the clouds move and the birds flying overhead. In the distance a plane leaves a jet stream. When you float, you can't hear anything, just the sound of silence. You need silence to enfold you and give you a sense of peace.

When you surrender control, you will find your intuition will heighten. You will know more at a soul level. You will be carrying less baggage. You will lighten up. Floating is the secret.

Love,
Mother

I took the advice seriously. Ray and I decided the only way I could float was to get out of town. We booked a condo in Jupiter, Florida, and drove south. There I'd get up at dawn to watch the sun rise over the ocean. Prayer felt natural. Meditation came easily. Writing in my journal became ritual. Still, it took weeks for me to breathe deeply. Following Mother's directions, every day I floated in the pool and my exhaustion started to lessen.

3/6/06

Dear Loanne,

This time of your life is very precious. You are focusing on the many gifts God has given you. Your attitude of gratitude is an important factor in the healing you are experiencing. It lifts you to a higher vibration and in doing so, it allows you to shed some of the guilt, criticism, and fear you collected over time. It also permits you to "see" your life and your potential more clearly. Being thankful for everything is key in lightening up your mind and therefore affecting your soul in a special way.

Like seeing the ripple on the ocean, it adds depth and dimension to what you see. As you release the heaviness of judgment, you will see the ripple of your life. Each loving act "hits" the shore eventually. Each loving comprehension gives a little "hug" to the sand eventually. As you watched the dark clouds lifting off the horizon, making "room" for the sunrise, you are releasing the dark clouds of Cyndi's life and death. You will see a glorious sunrise, I promise.

It is important to relax and just be. It gives your body and mind and spirit an opportunity to rebalance. It gives you a chance to shed more negativity. It gives you focus on who you are and what you want. It sheds the barnacles and lightens the "boat" of your body. Don't rush your mind to the future. Stay in this moment. Enjoy this time, this day. Stay in the moment and you will hear and respond to the guidance you are receiving.

You have much help these days. All your needs are being cared for. Enjoy whatever moments you can and float through the sadness until it washes over you like a wave. Then float again. You are being held in the palm of God's hand.

Lovingly,
Mother

The more I journaled with Mother and Cyndi, the lighter I felt by the day. By the time we left Florida, I was committed to two things: forgiveness and the power of celestial conversations.

CHAPTER SEVEN

The Transpersonal Path

For the next four years, I traversed the hills and valleys of my hope and grief. Some days I was too tired to do basic things. Other days I was energized but had no idea what to do. At times I felt I'd fallen from a boat into an ocean at night. Panic set in before hope loomed, only to disappear in a fog of confusion. For human understanding, I turned to my grief counselor and The Compassionate Friends. For spiritual understanding, I turned to my journals.

Mother's entries expanded with information about her own life, but on the related themes of forgiveness and disconnection:

4/15/06

When I was alive I didn't understand the power of forgiveness, but believe me it is the most powerful tool of human beings. Don't underestimate the intention of forgiveness. Just be willing to forgive every little thing: The way someone speaks to you or doesn't; the way someone ignores you; the way someone gives you unwelcome advice; the way someone judges you. Every little thing forgiven takes away a piece of the huge boulder that weighs so heavily on your heart.

When I was alive, I collected items to be forgiven and held them as my personal treasure. I couldn't let go. What a waste! I'm telling you, from my heart, don't collect injustices. Let each one go like picking weeds from a garden...

6/7/06

Dear Loanne,

Your name, as you write it, expresses the disconnection that you feel. Your given name, Lois, brings up much of our relationship that went awry. Please forgive me for not being the loving and nurturing Mother you wanted me to be. You chose me. I chose you. Our inability to overcome intimacy in our relationship is a significant reason for you to overcome your own inability to be intimate with those you love. I don't think I ever had an intimate moment in my lifetime. I hungered for it as much as you do, but my fear of intimacy was larger than my hunger for it, and each one cancelled out the other.

Fear is the biggest obstacle to living life fully. If there is any "gift" I've given you, Loanne, it is the instruction book on how fear kills relationships stone-cold dead. As you discover surrender and forgiveness, look also at the FEAR you carry. You are so much more courageous than I ever was, but the core of fear in you is still a stumbling block to your becoming all you can be.

Give your fears to God. He/She/It knows that fear is trash that clutters our minds — nothing more. The fear of what could happen or the fear of losing control or the fear of an unknown stops the mind from thinking and the body from functioning. Turn over each fear to God. I kept swallowing down my fears until my stomach literally swelled up like a balloon. I thought no one would notice. The truth be told, everyone noticed.

You are much further along than I was at your age. I will help you continue to surpass me because you are not only my daughter, you are my star-pupil whom I love and admire deeply. Continue to release any "trash" that you find and your journey will be lighter and brighter and filled with love.

Love,
Mother

As the months passed, my life did lighten. Many days resentment sloughed off me like dead skin. I even began speaking to friends about the journals. Intrigued, they encouraged me to write a book about them. I resisted.

"My journals are too personal to be in a book," I replied.

But the persistent interest of others pressured me to review all six journals I had at that time — three with Mother, three with Cyndi. In their pages I read the story of my own transformation, starting with the pain and anger that had enveloped me on the very first page. I thought, *What if my experience could help another person? Wouldn't that make the whole grief journey worthwhile?*

I asked a regional author and writing teacher I respect if she thought this type of journaling could help others. The teacher said it had promise. Cyndi agreed so heartily that she produced a title, *Celestial Conversations*.

1/10/07

The celestial conversations we have had over the last 1½ years are enough to show you that it is possible to penetrate the wall of silence that most people have perceived is erected at the moment of death. If we could give people the tools to penetrate that wall, to understand that it is an illusion, we can be giving the gift of life to relationships that need healing.

I began a book outline and took it to a writer's retreat in a mansion on Long Beach Island, New Jersey. Twenty writers attended. One was a friend who pressured me to share my idea with the ladies in attendance. Still I resisted and asked Mother if the time was right. Her response was more than I anticipated:

10/10/08

Loanne – you are so right. Now is the time, not just to write your book, but to pull together all of your understanding and evolve into the Wise Woman You Are!

With those celestial blessings, I quelled my trepidation and told the ladies in the group about my story and celestial inspirations. It was the first time I'd shared with total strangers, and their encouragement was rapid and complete. With their attention and questions, they showed genuine interest and immediately thought of how they could apply the process to their own lives. My confidence grew so much that I shared my plans with people in The Compassionate Friends and The International Women's Writing Guild, a nonprofit organization dedicated to the empowerment of women through writing. Some people offered to help me while others wanted to know when the book became available so they could buy it for friends and family.

Many people said communicating with souls beyond the veil was not only a possibility but a daily occurrence. But the question for me was whether I could inspire people to try *Celestial Conversations* as a practical tool for healing. Mother wrote:

11/29/08

Oh honey, this wasn't the first time you doubted, but who's counting? Doubt isn't a bad thing. It pushes you past your stuck places by putting it on the table as an issue.

As God is my witness, this is real! More than that, it is important, not just for you and me, but for many…

Sharing my personal journals and gathering support was one thing, but facing the potential negative judgments and skepticism of strangers was another. Enter Dr. George-Harold Jennings, Drew University psychology professor and author of *Passages Beyond the Gate*, a scholarly and award-winning book making the case that spirituality, including transpersonal communication and inspiration, is a living and important element in American psychology.

A friend introduced me to Dr. Jennings and the springboard for his work, which is based on the idea that the science of psychology has not yet drawn or explained all the boundaries of human consciousness. Some states of consciousness historically defined as mental illness, for example, actually are simply unknown territory—a psychological frontier, if you will. Instead of being psychotic, some states are healthy, even transcendent, which is to say they may allow a person to access supernatural guidance.

Ready to learn more, I met with Dr. Jennings in the hope he'd help me find a way to describe my celestial conversations as something other than channeling. I didn't feel like a medium and had no interest in contacting entities for other people. I also was eager to find out what transpersonal psychology was. I had never heard the term. At least I thought I hadn't.

Excited about this new development, I wrote in Mother's journal:

1/2/09

Hi Mom!

Today I am meeting with Dr. Jennings. I want a partner, tutor, listener to help me with my book. I miss your presence today. I would call you, if I could. I am so glad to have this means of communication. I feel that it fills a gap that I would never have otherwise. I want to give that gift to others.

I met Dr. Jennings in his office at Sycamore Cottage on the university campus in Madison, New Jersey. Cold rain dripped down my neck as I closed my umbrella on the front porch of the little white cottage. In Dr. Jennings's office on the first floor, books overflowed the desk, table, and bookcases. When he stood to shake my hand, he towered over the stained glass lamp on his desk and his head almost touched the low ceiling. This gentle giant of a man contained the key to my spiritual growth as well as perspective for *Celestial Conversations*. I knew it immediately.

His bright eyes and smile made me comfortable as I summarized how I began my journaling with Mother and Cyndi after they died. Without blinking an eye, he leaned across his desk and shared he'd had a special interest in transpersonal psychology dating back to 1979 and his days as a graduate student in clinical psychology at Pennsylvania State University. He went on to explore it further at Yale University.

"In those days spirituality and psychology were far apart in their understanding of human beings," Dr. Jennings explained. "Transpersonal psychology presented a bridge between the two. I started writing *Passages* in 1996 for students enrolled in my psychology courses here at Drew. The book, based upon Jungian respect for intuition, dreams, meditation, and other mystical aspects of human beings, makes a strong case for integrating transpersonal psychology with the more accepted types of psychology."

Dr. Jennings wasn't alone in his interest. He belongs to the Association for Transpersonal Psychology, a member-supported organization founded in 1971 that coordinates scientific, social, and clinical transpersonal work across the globe. It publishes *The Journal of Transpersonal Psychology* featuring articles supporting worldwide interest in the field. Dr. Jennings offered me a few copies so I could read them at home.

An invisible door opened for me. Emphasizing I'd never heard of transpersonal psychology, I asked him to help me understand how it related to my journaling. He picked up a copy of *Passages*, thumbed through its pages, and read: "Transpersonal psychology offers itself as one type of solution to the existentialist's search for meaning. It offers, among other things, the spiritual path or path of entry to higher realms of being, knowing, and communicating."

"Communicating?" I said. *Was it possible I'd just found a wider way to describe my transpersonal journaling than the metaphysical term "channeling"? Could my book and method draw readers interested not only in the metaphysical world, but also in the spiritual and psychological worlds?*

Dr. Jennings invited me to visit again to further our discussion, and I promised to return whenever he had time to meet me. Still wrestling with the meaning of transpersonal psychology when I arrived home, I went directly to my first journal with Mother before I took off my coat. On page one I'd written:

2/22/05

I do believe that conversation through writing can help us both to soothe pain and open up immense possibilities in the transpersonal state.

Eyes bulging, I read the sentence again. There was the word "transpersonal" written by my own hand four years earlier. I turned the page to my mother's first letter to me.

2/25/05

> *Now I see that you know that communication and love can be shared transpersonally.*

I couldn't wait to go back to visit with Dr. Jennings so I made an appointment. In the meantime, I traced the beginnings of transpersonal psychology. After incubating in the humanistic psychology wave for a number of decades, it became its own school of thought in the 1960s, scant years before I was journaling with the intention of finding help for Ray Jr. in 1975. How I wish I'd known that!

The term "transpersonal psychology," though, reportedly was first used by William James, author of *The Varieties of Religious Experience: A Study in Human Nature*, during one of his lectures at Harvard University near the turn of the twentieth century. But James, a doctor, psychologist, and philosopher interested in the psychology of mysticism and other religious experiences, was but one father of the field. Others also were men of medicine and psychology, including Carl Jung, with his emphasis on dreams and the human subconscious; Abraham Maslow, who was interested in peak human experiences; and Viktor Frankl, whose work covered existential analysis and the human search for meaning.

It was Frankl and Stanislav Grof, a pioneer researcher in non-ordinary states of consciousness, who suggested that "transpersonal psychology" should be the name for the emerging field that was the wide nexus of all their work.

Many institutions worldwide now offer master's degrees and doctorates in transpersonal psychology, described as a full-spectrum psychology. For instance, the Institute of Transpersonal Psychology in Palo Alto, California calls the field "a serious scholarly interest in the immanent and transcendent dimensions of human experience," including genius, mysticism, and exceptional achievements.

Often transpersonal psychology is confused with paranormal studies, which focus on psychic phenomena. The two are quite different. While transpersonal psychology may in some instances take paranormal studies into account, its fundamental goal is to study people, not bent spoons or ghosts.

I met with Dr. Jennings often for several years, soaking up his knowledge and reassurances.

"Lo Anne, transpersonal psychologists are no longer classifying experiences like yours as a psychological crisis," he said, "but as a spiritual experience that can be studied, just like near-death experiences are being investigated."

Never once in all our meetings did he express any doubt I was in touch with my mother and daughter. The fact they were both dead presented no impediment to our conversation. Indeed it made our talks more interesting. In fact, Dr. Jennings shared his own intuitive abilities and opened a horizon of possibility.

"After decades of research into psychic phenomena, consciousness studies, and transpersonal phenomena," he stated, "I now have the theoretical knowledge to understand and explain many of my own psychic and transpersonal experiences, and in many cases, the psychic and transpersonal experiences of other people. I have come to realize that I am an empath."

"What is an empath?" I asked.

"One who is very sensitive and capable of readily tuning into the emotions of other people, even to the point of experiencing the emotions or coming very close to experiencing the emotions felt by others," he said. "As a psychotherapist, this skill is especially useful."

Reflecting on Dr. Jennings's words, I realized that his empathic skill is one of the reasons he listened so intently to my story. He also seemed to feel the healing that had become the fabric of my life through my celestial conversations.

In turn, our talks helped him open more to his own gifts and talents. As life would have it, Dr. Jennings lost his mother and sister during the first three years of our meetings. Generously, he shared with me an astounding empathic personal experience in which he witnessed his sister's death from a distance.

"Two days following the passing of my sister, Shirley," he said, "my ability as an empath was greatly amplified just before sunrise. I felt a strong, almost overwhelming feeling of anxiety. Even though my eyes were closed, I was not sleeping. I was not dreaming. I was in an altered state of awareness, somewhere between the state of sleep and being awake. No dream I have ever had felt like the experience, not even a lucid dream.

"I could think clearly and I questioned myself, *Why am I feeling this anxiety? I have no reason to feel this level of anxiety.*"

It occurred to him, he said, that the anxiety was not his. Rather, it belonged to his sister. The instant her name entered his awareness, he had a strong sense of both being his sister and watching her death unfolded.

"My sister wondered what was happening," he explained. "She turned around and saw a light, and in the light she saw a face that instantaneously brought calmness and radiated a sense of peacefulness throughout her entire being. When she recognized Christ, the anxiety immediately left her. And it left me. Even as I felt this, I observed it. I not only physically and empathically experienced an aspect of my sister crossing over, I also saw it unfold from a distance. Given that in my reality, the event had already occurred, I had observed the unfolding of a past event."

Like his sister, Dr. Jennings also was aware of the presence of other people in the light. Like her, he did not discern the faces but did hear a voice lovingly call, "Shirley Mae."

Dr. Jennings had observed his sister's death spiritually; I had observed my mother's passing physically. But both of us had discovered that the death of loved ones brought to us an unusual gift of grace, not to mention a palpable understanding of the blessings of death.

All over the world professional people like Dr. Jennings and ordinary people like me are exploring and pushing the boundaries of spirit, at least as mankind conventionally defines them today. Researchers in Sweden, England, and Australia have started scientifically investigating phenomena such as my journaling, and here in the United States the University of Virginia in Charlottesville has begun delving into the possibility of life after death.

The phenomenon of journaling with loved ones in spirit, however, is extremely difficult to study using scientific protocol, according to Robert Ginsberg, founder and vice president of the Forever Family Foundation, an organization devoted to using science and spirituality to explore the afterlife while comforting the bereaved.

"Unlike mediumship studies where specific information can be scored and evaluated," Ginsberg said, "channeled accounts tend to be more general and seem to be mainly focused on wisdom and existence in the afterlife."

The idea of scientific research dazzles me, but my faith is important to me, too. All my life I've identified strongly with being a traditional, Catholic woman. Frankly, I was intimidated by religious people who might condemn me because I had the hubris to believe I could discern and connect with spiritual forces without the aid of an intermediary.

On the other hand, I was aware of the deep mystical literature of my own tradition. Many Catholic saints have communicated with disembodied beings, including Joan of Arc and Hildegard of Bingen. Of course, they were saints. I am definitely not. Nevertheless, I found myself wondering what the transpersonal psychologists of today would learn about Catherine of Siena if they were to study her abilities.

I also was aware my journals were helping me heal and increasing my compassion. In the end, all religions seem to agree that effect is the true test of any spiritual belief. Most of my life I have been a student of spirituality of all types. For thirty years I've read from the library of Edgar Cayce's Association for Research and Enlightenment in Virginia. There and elsewhere I've learned about meditation, auras, dreams, psychic experiences, and past lives.

All my studies and experiences, including my Catholicism, have become a tapestry of my spiritual and religious life, and I am grateful for every thread because each has given me a broad awareness of God's many gifts to humans in general and me in particular. In my years with Dr. Jennings I came to accept my transpersonal journaling with Mother and Cyndi as a golden thread. Through my mother and daughter I learned the human state is only one part of a soul's life. Death is another. And so it is. A soul retains its essence and changes its form, just as water can transform into ice or steam.

CHAPTER EIGHT

New Karma

When I started each of my journals, I didn't see a way to true peace, but I was willing to search for it. Mother wrote:

2/28/06

The peace of God is the ultimate goal for everyone. I never found it on Earth. However, if anyone can, you can. Very few humans make that goal important to them. You are ahead of the game. Very few people ask for help to achieve that goal. They search, but forget help is at their fingertips. You are aware. Very few people on your path recognize how lovely and important a gift it is to be asked to help another human being

*achieve their goal before they cross over. Everyone
(here) benefits as we all work to support your
journey. If only everyone on earth knew how
much could be achieved by working towards a
common goal: The Peace of God.*

*Love,
Mother*

All these years later I can say I've found peace in
a most unlikely place—the knowledge that, with a
healing intention, incarnate and discarnate souls
can keep loving each other and helping each other
grow. The soul on Earth gains by letting go anger,
guilt, and criticism about the person who has
passed. The soul beyond the veil gains by helping
a human being release negativity. According to
Mother, cooperation through celestial conversations is one of many ways to balance karma that
otherwise would manifest in either soul's next lifetime. At the very least the conversations can help
relieve negative karma on either side of the veil.

Though Mother and I had never discussed karma in her lifetime, our journaling gave us an opportunity to do so. In my thirties I'd been introduced
to the concept by an astrologer friend of my mother. Clayre had graduated Smith College, was High
Episcopalian, and so fashionable she looked as
though she'd stepped out of *Harper's Bazaar*. She
traveled to lecture and prepared astrological charts.
Mother first met Clayre at a local museum where
she gave a talk about the astrology chart for the

United States based on the date the Continental Congress adopted the Declaration of Independence — July 4, 1776. Then and there Clayre offered to do the charts of anyone whose birthday was on or near July 4. Since Mother's birthday was July 3, she got one. The information was so helpful to Mother that she had charts done for Ray and me as birthday gifts. Shocked that my mother, who received Communion daily, would give us astrology charts, we thought they must be something special.

In 1978, after Clayre had done charts on three of our children, Mother introduced me to her. At that point I'd listened to five separate charts of family members and developed a respect for astrology. Clayre became my teacher and a friend with whom I could talk about any metaphysical subject.

When I questioned her about astrology running contrary to my Catholic beliefs, she laughed and said, "Lo Anne, didn't you know the three wise men were astrologers?" She also quoted Mark 8:27-29:

> *And Jesus went on with His disciples to the villages of Caesarea Philippi; and on the way He asked His disciples, Who do people say that I am?*

> *And they answered Him, John the Baptist; and others say, Elijah; but others, one of the prophets.*

> *And He asked them, But who do you yourselves say that I am? Peter replied to Him, You are the Christ (the Messiah, the Anointed One).*

"The great religious leaders that were named by Christ's apostles in this passage were dead at the time, Lo Anne," Clayre explained. "That's one of the few verses in the Bible that refers to reincarnation. Remember the Christian churches have had many writers and censors as the Gospels were being recorded and reprinted over the centuries."

That conversation inspired my twenty-year investigation into reincarnation. Clayre also claimed Ray and I had shared a lifetime in Atlantis, a legendary island that sank into the ocean in ancient times, according to some accounts. Plato was the first to allude to Atlantis in his writings. Though we'd never contemplated past lives, Ray and I shared a curiosity about Atlantis and had watched many television shows about it.

Clayre's main interest in astrology was accentuating the gifts and talents each soul brought to earth as a baby. My astrological chart showed that I possessed healing ability.

"It will take many years for you to develop into the healer you will become," Clayre told me. "You might as well get started."

It was Clayre who introduced me to the work and library of Edgar Cayce, the famed psychic healer who died in the 1940s. Though I had five children under seven years old, I made time to read the Cayce books about psychics, past lives, and the universal ring of knowledge. I also absorbed information about natural foods, herbs, and many forms of healing. I often called Clayre to ask about metaphysical subjects—karma in particular. One of her examples deeply affected me the rest of my life.

She believed the thalidomide children born in the 1960s, particularly in Germany, were reincarnated Gestapo members who had maimed others and chosen to return as maimed children to balance their karma. In her view, a murderer in one life might return as a victim in another, just as an abuser might come back as a victim of abuse.

"That is exactly what I would do if I were God!" I exclaimed.

My God was a loving God. What could be more loving than to ask someone who made mistakes in one lifetime: "Do you want to go back to Earth to fully experience the effects of your mistake?" For me, Clayre's view opened a new understanding of "an eye for an eye."

Our discussions forced me to think deeply about karma. Over time, I became a believer, but in all my metaphysical travels I'd never come across the concept of karma as occurring in any way but through living successive lives. In our journaling, however, Mother was saying there are many ways to balance the karma of a soul and that successive death and rebirth was only one. She was saying the dead and the living can help each other.

Why not? If God created many galaxies, surely he easily could create many forms of karma. Perhaps the traditional Catholic cosmology—heaven, hell, and purgatory—was just one. I respected the idea immediately.

Researching Mother's words led me to Spiritism, a set of beliefs based on the understanding of karma as the condition of a soul, incarnate or discarnate. In the mid-nineteenth century French educator Hippolyte Léon Denizard Rivail, who authored the *Spiritist Codification* under the *nom de plume* Allan Kardec, wrote that love, which is all there is, penetrates the veil in both directions. Love inspires both the living and dead to forgive each other so their souls can grow closer to God.

In *Spirits' Book*, a part of his *Codification* published in London in 1898, Kardec also suggested that a wrong committed during a human life could cause moral pain in the afterlife. Throughout the *Spirits' Book* he asks specific questions of spirits. One is: "When a spirit says that he suffers, what is the nature of the suffering he feels?" The answer is: "Mental anguish, which causes him tortures far more painful than any physical sufferings."

Kardec goes on to state that "we know that spirits possess perception, sensation, hearing, sight and that these faculties are attributes of their whole being, and not, as in men, of part of their being.... They hear the sound of our voice, and yet are able to understand us, without the help of speech, by the mere transmission of thought."

I had written similar words in my journals from both my mother and my daughter. It makes sense to me that if a soul (or perispirit, as Kardec refers to a person who has died) is given the opportunity to review his life and sees his own mistakes, he would feel the pain of regret. Both Mother and Cyndi have expressed great regret for the things they didn't do or didn't say in their mortal lives. In many letters they have asked my forgiveness, which tells me their perispirits feel a negative reaction to some aspects of their life review.

So, too, do I deeply regret actions I did not take when they were alive. To this day I feel the mental anguish of losing our daughter and wonder how I might have prevented it. In my own religious faith, we would call this experience purgatory.

Kardec writes of angels, prayers, reincarnation, and the mercy and kindness of a loving God. In *Book II*, this passage jumped off the page into my heart: "Besides, you must remember that what appears to you to be a misfortune is not always such: for the good which it is destined to work out is often greater than the seeming evil. This fact is not always recognized by you, because you are too apt to think only of the present moment, and of your own immediate satisfaction."

When Mother and Cyndi died, I most certainly was thinking of the present moment. I am now, however, aware that their deaths, though tragic, have opened me to an afterlife filled with love and wisdom—a universe that I only suspected existed. Though I don't agree with everything Kardec proposes, I have to affirm he has tapped into the same field of knowledge I continue to find in the kindness and compassion of Mother and Cyndi.

In one celestial conversation Cyndi wrote that she forgot pacts she made before she reincarnated. But don't we all? Even if a soul comes back to balance karma, the person in whom that soul resides will not remember the contract because free will is essential to human life. If people knew the outcome of their lives, they'd be playing parts. Kardec writes: "Nothing comes to pass without the permission of God, for it is He who has established all the laws that rule the universe."

According to Kardec, God gives each spirit the freedom to choose along with the responsibility of those choices.

"The right road is open to him as freely as the wrong road," Kardec writes. "But if he succumbs there still remains to him the consoling fact that all is not over with him and that God in His goodness allows him to recommence the task which he has done badly (through reincarnation)."

One day my daughter Karen called and said, "Mom, I think you better sit down." She handed the phone to her eight-year-old son, who made a most unusual, matter-of-fact declaration. He said Aunt Cyndi would be born again in 2009. Surprised I didn't know, he repeated himself, this time including the date and place. I didn't want to believe my grandson. I felt afraid and confused as I tried to keep our conversation light. He'd just given me a lot of information about karma and reincarnation, and I didn't feel comfortable with any of it. I turned to Mother in our journal. She responded:

Feb 3, 2009

We all have new territory to cross. Cyndi's decision is critical to her soul. She needs our help now more than ever. She has mine and I know she will have yours, even though you don't understand or really approve. Your fear as her earthly mother needs to be released now. Cyndi needs to clear her karma and time is of the essence for her to do that.

I know that she is determined. She has sought out all the guidance, strength and angelic-help she can, in order to complete her mission this time. Constant prayer will help, especially from you. Just pray for her highest good. Don't think too much about where she is going or how it will work. If there was ever a time to trust your guidance, this is the time. Truly the story of Abraham crossing the desert should be your example. Trust God to lead you through this desert. I have rallied the troops and we will surround Cyndi with loving spiritual support. Trust us. Trust her. Trust God.

Lovingly,
Mother

Then I turned to Cyndi, asking directly if she was returning to earth.

Feb. 3, 2009

Yes it is true, Mom. I have to get back to an earthly form for many reasons. I really messed up my karma when I took the overdose of medication. It is essential to my soul that I come back and balance the scale.

I'm scared, too. I had great intentions the last time, but I couldn't fulfill my mission. I am stronger than ever in my intention to do God's work and I have picked a situation that will help me grow in my mission and my good karma. I need you to keep me in prayer until you leave the planet. Then you will see for yourself how we did.

I am counting on you to keep me in prayer. I am told that I can stay connected with you because we have established such a bond. The connection seems simple enough, but then everything seems logical and simple from here.

I know Grandma, Uncle Artie, and my angels will help me. That's why I have chosen a very spiritual person to be my mother. One who encourages spirit. If we all intend to stay connected, I am convinced it can be done. Love conquers all, Mom, and I love you more than words can express.

Love,
Cyndi

I prayed and kept journaling as Cyndi's supposed rebirth came to pass. For almost a month after the predicted date of her return, I didn't journal with her. I couldn't. I was as nervous as if I were the birth mother. Then on March 11, 2009:

> *I am grateful for your prayers. It was a long journey. Funny how we forget the basics. So many times we come to Earth — almost always the same way. And yet we forget a lot of things. Birth is so hard, even when it's classified an easy birth. Still the shock of it is enormous. No words or means of communication to share with those caring for you. That's huge! And one of the reasons I need you right now as much as you need me. Stay with me, Mom!*

> *Love,*
> *Cyndi*

I did. Our journaling during her transition back to Earth helped me to grow and love her in ways I never thought possible. Continuing my journaling with Cyndi, though, has been a lesson in trust. I still grapple with how she could reincarnate and still journal with me about her boys and helping her family. I asked her and she replied:

2/19/11

> *Mom, the same way you are connected to all members of our family. When you are writing or driving or playing golf, you can tune in to Karen or Diane or any of your children or grandchildren. It's not that hard. The Love-Connection allows me to go to the "website" and*

open up that portal. It gives me total focus and concentration. Love is the "computer" that allows me to connect. I think that is the easiest translation: Love for and from my family, friends, and even former enemies allows me to connect when called by their memories, sadness, guilt, or questions. Intention on both sides allows the connection quite easily.

Love,
Cyndi

I learned from my daughter precious lessons about how a soul enters into a baby's body, forgetful of its mission but dedicated to the opportunity to grow through the human experience. In the two years since her rebirth, I welcomed three more grandchildren, making a total of thirteen at this writing. Learning from Cyndi how much the babies really know and are unable to express made my role as grandmother even more of an honor.

More than ever, I used Reiki, mental telepathy, and prayer to soothe the precious souls who came into my family. They are all part of the special generations of children who have come to Earth to restore balance, spread love, and bring healing into the world. I watched and supported these little ones as their healing light and intuitive gifts combined with my own. We talk about angels and fairies, dreams and fears, animals and ghosts in ways I never could have done with my children. I see powerful determination, extraordinary intelligence, and strength in these wee ones, even in the cradle.

I've felt fortunate to have my mother and daughter to help me believe in God's plan for healing the planet. Through the years I've visited the cemetery. I like to sit on the bench by Our Lady of Lourdes next to Cyndi's grave. When I go, I pray for strength and the fortitude to be a light in these dark times. I thank my mother for showing me how beautiful death can be, as well as giving me the solace of our celestial conversations. I thank our daughter for leading me through the shock of grief into enormous gratitude for having been a part of her life then and now.

Sometimes I bring a journal with me to read and reflect. Opening to a page at random one day, I read Cyndi's message from July 19, 2006:

> *As you go through this day, please remember the good times, the laughter and the love. It was also there. Just because the end of my life was so dark and tragic, don't color my life with tragedy. Overall, it was good. I had my wonderful siblings and my beautiful boys, and my dear, loving parents. If I could have focused on that, my life would have taken a different course. Focus for me, Mom. Help everyone, especially my boys. Remember the love we shared, not the pain and sorrow. It's only love that matters, only love that crosses the divide of life and death, only love that lives through eternity.*

Tears rolled down my face as a butterfly landed on the impatiens I had planted in front of her headstone. None of this is about death, I realized. All of this is about how karma shapes our lives and how love transcends all. Ours is a love story that deserved to be written, and I was the lucky one who became a pencil in God's hand.

Acknowledgments

First, I am filled with gratitude to God for allowing me to live long enough to expand my understanding of life and death. Such unconditional love for humanity, until now, has been impossible for me to grasp. I also offer thanks:

To my mother, who taught me important lessons during her life and opened my portal to the world beyond the veil as a result of her death;

To my daughter Cyndi, who gave me the ultimate reason to explore the meaning of forgiveness and unconditional love;

To my daughter Karen, who believed her grandmother and her sister could journal with me and offered to help me share my experience with the world;

To my daughter-in-law Crystal, for her commitment to helping me build and maintain a website;

To my entire family for encouraging me to see the possibilities of writing *Celestial Conversations* and, in their grief, serving as its first audience as they lived out their grief journeys;

To my editor and friend, Lorraine Ash, who carefully molded my words and ideas into the book you see today. Her encouragement and talent made all the difference;

To Bill Ash, whose manuscript and book designs helped my dream take such a beautiful form;

To those who participated in the Celestial Circles workshops in New Jersey and Texas, who shared their ideas and supported my intention to be clear and healing as I wrote this book;

To Dr. George-Harold Jennings, who generously shared his time and expertise on transpersonal psychology with me, while believing in *Celestial Conversations* as a tool for grieving hearts;

To The International Women's Writing Guild, which gave me a nest while I contemplated writing *Celestial Conversations*. I am especially indebted to two member authors, Susan Tiberghien and Julie Genovese, who encouraged me to continue through the pain of writing my first book;

Acknowledgments

To the Scriveners, my writing group, who gave me the space to continuously write for seven years. I am especially indebted to Ethel Miller, Jean Pfeffer, and Elizabeth Barrett for their consistent support and love;

To those unnamed angels who helped me stay committed to bringing this story to the world, especially those who offered to walk with me along the way. Namaste.

About the Author

L o Anne Mayer has studied various forms of healing for thirty years. Raising her six children inspired her to learn about nutrition, charismatic healing, therapeutic touch, the mind-body connection, and various forms of meditation.

She is a student of *A Course in Miracles* and Edgar Cayce as well as a Reiki master. For twelve years she taught Louise Hay's *Healing Your Life* course.

Inspired by her training with Alma Daniel to teach *Angel Meditation*, Lo Anne produced and hosted a television show entitled *Angels at Work*, which emphasized the good works of ordinary people. She also wrote and presented her own course, *Choosing Joy: How to Create a Joy-filled Life*.

Today she is committed to helping others discover that love between two people can be shared and relationships healed even after one of them dies. She facilitates Celestial Circles designed to inspire and facilitate written exchanges between those in grief and their departed loved ones.

She lives in New Jersey with her husband, Dr. Raymond Mayer.

Celestial Conversations is her first book.

Learn More

Start a Celestial Conversations journal

Celestial Conversations: A guided journey, by Lo Anne Mayer, features instructions and thirty days' worth of designed journaling pages sprinkled with quotations from the author's own journals.

Visit www.CapeHouseBooks.com to purchase and download *Celestial Conversations: A guided journey.*

Participate in a Celestial Circle

Lo Anne Mayer leads small Celestial Circles in the New York Metro and Austin areas and also makes special appearances at conferences and other gatherings nationwide.

Visit www.CelestialConversations.com to view Lo Anne's calendar of events.

Connect with Lo Anne Mayer

Write to the author to share your experiences with your own celestial conversations, ask a question, or arrange a Skype session for your bereavement group or book club.

Visit www.CelestialConversations.com to contact Lo Anne.